12

2.

'The Appetite and the Eye'

'The Appetite and the Eye'

*Visual aspects of
food and its presentation
within their
historic context*

EDITED BY C. ANNE WILSON

with illustrations by
Peter Brears

Edinburgh University Press

Papers from the Second Leeds Symposium
on Food History and Traditions,
April 1987, with additional papers

© C. Anne Wilson, 1991
Edinburgh University Press
22 George Square, Edinburgh

Set in Berthold Garamond
by Hislop & Day Limited, Edinburgh
and printed in Great Britain by
The Alden Press Limited, Oxford

British Library Cataloguing
in Publication Data
The Appetite and the eye:
visual aspects of food and its presentation
within their historic context.
1. Food. Visual presentation, history
I. Wilson, C. Anne (Constance Anne). II. Series
641.3

ISBN 0 7486 0101 5

Contents

About the contributors

List of illustrations

1.

Introduction

I

2.

Ritual, Form and Colour in the Mediaeval Food Tradition

C. ANNE WILSON

5

3.

From Mediaeval Great Hall to Country-house Dining-
room: the Furniture and Setting of the Social Meal

C. ANNE WILSON

28

4.

Decoration of the Tudor and Stuart Table

PETER BREARS

56

5.

Ideal Meals and their Menus from the Middle Ages to the
Georgian Era

C. ANNE WILSON

98

6.

Keeping Up Appearances: the Genteel Art of Dining in
Middle-class Victorian Britain

DENA ATTAR

123

Contents

7.

Illusion and Illustration in Cookery-books since the 1940s
LYNETTE HUNTER

141

Index
161

List of illustrations

1. Dining in 'a chamber with a chimney' (from British Library MS Add. 24098, fol. 19v.).
2. Court cupboard, walnut, *c.* 1600.
3. Joined stool, oak, late sixteenth century.
4. Side table, mahogany, *c.* 1730.
5. Side table, urns, pedestals and wine cooler, made by Thomas Chippendale *c.* 1776.
6. A family taking tea, 1732.
7. Pottery salts: three examples from the mid-sixteenth to early seventeenth century.
8. Silver salts: four examples made between 1493 and 1685.
9. Napkin folding, 1682: how to form a Cockleshell Double, a cross, and a cross of Lorraine.
10. Spoons: four examples made between 1526 and 1696.
11. Knives: five examples made between *c.* 1530 and *c.* 1710.
12. Forks: five examples made between *c.* 1670 and *c.* 1710.
13. Wooden trencher of *c.* 1600, and pewter trencher of the 1690s.
14. Delftware plates: three examples of the mid- to late seventeenth century.
15. Pewter charger made probably in the 1660s.
16. Delftware chargers: two examples, one made in 1600, the other in 1635.
17. Slipware chargers: two examples, one made by Thomas Toft probably in the 1670s, the other made in North Devon, *c.* 1650–75.
18. Table diagram from P. Lamb, *Royal Cookery; or The Complete Court-Cook,* 1710.
19. A table-setting recreated.
20. Dish ring, made by Samuel Hood, 1697.

21. Garnishing: the grand salad.
22. Ewer and basin, silver gilt, 1617.
23. Early French table diagram from M. Audiger, *La Maison Reglée*, 1692.
24. (a) and (b): Two tables, with arrangements of dishes for 6 diners and for 14 or 15 diners, from F. Massialot, *The Court and Country Cook*, 1702.
25. English table diagram from H. Howard, *England's Newest Way in All Sorts of Cookery*, 3rd ed., 1710.
26. Table-setting for a two-course dinner in December, from C. Carter, *The Compleat City and Country Cook* 1732.
27. Table-setting for a two-course dinner in September, from *The Whole Duty of a Woman*, 1737.
28. Table-setting for a two-course dinner in winter, from E. Smith, *The Compleat Housewife*, 1727.
29. Table-setting for a dinner in May, from M. Bradley, *The British Housewife*, vol. 1, 1737.
30. Bills of fare and verbal instructions from *The Complete Family Piece*, 1736.
31. Dishes laid out in order in the kitchen, ready to be served into the dining-room, from A. Chambers, *The Ladies Best Companion*, c. 1800.
32. Table diagram and accompanying menu from *The Modern Method of Regulating and Forming a Table*, 1760.
33. Eel with Montpelier butter.
34. Sheep's ears in croustade.
35. Croquettes, gateaux, cotelettes, matelote.
36. Table plan for *Diner à la Russe*.
37. *Diner à la Russe:* half-table for eighteen.
38. Trifle, ices and jellies around.

About the contributors

DENA ATTAR is a Tutor-Counsellor at the Open University and lectures in Education. She previously taught English and Drama and carried out research into domestic manuals for the *Bibliography of Household Books*. She has published a number of articles, including some on the theme of women and cookery.

PETER BREARS is the Director of Leeds City Museums. He combines his interests in archaeology, architecture and the traditional food of Northern England with a great deal of practical experience of recreating the culinary confections of earlier centuries.

LYNETTE HUNTER is a Lecturer at the University of Leeds' Institute of Bibliography and Textual Criticism. She has published several books and articles on modern English literature, and is general editor of *Household and Cookery Books Published in Britain 1800-1914*

ANNE WILSON has worked for many years in the Brotherton Library of the University of Leeds, becoming involved in food history as a result of cataloguing the John Preston Collection of early English cookery-books. This led her to write *Food and Drink in Britain from the Stone Age to Recent Times*. She is currently researching the very early history of distilling.

1.

Introduction

In recent years the fashion for nouvelle cuisine has
highlighted the idea that food becomes more appetising
if it is made to look decorative. But this view is in fact very
old, and the papers gathered in this book explore some of
the ways in which both the appearance of food and its
surroundings have contributed to please the eye and
enhance the appetite of the eater during earlier periods of
our history.

A significant example of visually interesting foodstuffs
and ambiences was the Tudor and Stuart banquet of
sweetmeats; and at the first Leeds Symposium on Food
History and Traditions held in April 1986 the banquet was
examined in detail. The papers given on that occasion
have now been published under the title of *Banquetting
Stuffe*.[1]

Gervase Markham's *The English Huswife*, first published
in 1615, set out to teach the 'housewife of the middling sort'
how things ought to be done. Under the heading
'Ordering of banquets' he wrote:

> Thus having showed you how to preserve,
> conserve, candy, and make pastes of all kinds, in
> which four heads consists of the whole art of
> banqueting dishes, I will now proceed to the
> ordering or setting forth of a banquet, wherein

you shall observe that march-panes have the first place, the middle place, and last place: your preserved fruits shall be dished up first, your pastes next, your wet suckets after them, then your dried suckets, then your marmalades and codiniacs, then your comfits of all kinds; next your pears, apples, wardens baked, raw or roasted, and your oranges and lemons sliced; and lastly your wafer-cakes. Thus you shall order them in the closet; but when they go to the table, you shall first send forth a dish made for show only, as beast, bird, fish, fowl, according to invention; then your marchpane, then preserved fruit, then a paste, then a wet sucket, then a dry sucket, marmalade, comfits, apples, pears, wardens, oranges and lemons sliced, and then wafers, and another dish of preserved fruits, and so consequently all the rest before: no two dishes of one kind going or standing together, and this will not only appear delicate to the eye, but invite the appetite with the much variety thereof.

It will be seen that the final part of this passage supplied the idea for the theme for the Second Leeds Symposium on Food History and Traditions held in April 1987, and likewise the title for this book. But the whole passage helped to shape the theme, because it makes clear that in the early seventeenth century people cared about the way their food was presented: that they liked it to look 'delicate to the eye', and that they believed that an interesting variety of foods attractively laid out would 'invite the appetite'.

Widening the theme we decided to look also at the rooms and furnishings which people have chosen at different periods of time to provide the ambience for their special feasts and social meals, and at the table-settings and tableware which they found suitable for the service and consumption of food and drink. We discovered that another recent concept, that of 'power lunching', is also far from new: for centuries people have used meals as a means of displaying both their social position and their personal power. And from the Middle Ages onwards, new fashions in foods and meal service spread from the court downwards through the social hierarchy because people were so eager to create the impression that they were a little bit further up the social scale than other members of their peer group.

The papers in this book, 'Keeping Up Appearances: the Genteel Art of Dining in Middle-class Victorian Britain', by Dena Attar; 'Decoration of the Tudor and Stuart Table', by Peter Brears; and 'Ritual, Form and Colour in the Mediaeval Food Tradition', by Anne Wilson, are all based on the talks given under those titles at the Second Leeds Symposium on Food History and Traditions held at the University of Leeds Adult Education Centre on 4th April 1987. As part of the Symposium, the audience was invited to try its hand at napkin-folding in the seventeenth-century fashion, and to visit an exhibition of eighteenth-century cookery-books selected from the collections of early cookery-books in the Brotherton Library, University of Leeds, by Lucy Steuart to illustrate the appearance of 'the Well-dressed Eighteenth-century Table'. It has not been possible to reproduce the relevant pages and plates from all the books shown there, but some of them may be seen at the end of the short article about menus in cookery-books from the fourteenth to the eighteenth century titled, 'Ideal Meals and their Menus'.

We are also very glad that Lynette Hunter's paper, 'Illusion and Illustration in Cookery-Books since the 1940s' appears here, and provides a twentieth-century conclusion to a group of papers spanning the period from the Middle Ages to Victorian times. It also builds further on a sub-theme suggested by some of the papers, which might be called 'The Appetite and the Mind's Eye', concerning the question of how far people are influenced by the mental perceptions aroused when they read menus or see illustrations in cookery-books.

The visual aspects of food, and the idea of food created by visual stimuli; the appearance of the surroundings of food, its tableware and room-furnishings, and the rituals of its service; the social implications of the style of both food and surroundings: these are some of the topics explored in the following papers. We hope people who are interested in the history of food will enjoy reading about its ambience and its image in times past.

C. Anne Wilson
Leeds
February 1989

Reference 1. *Banquetting Stuffe: the Fare and Social Background of the Tudor and Stuart Grand Final Course,* edited by C. Anne Wilson, Edinburgh University Press, 1989.

2.

Ritual, Form and Colour in the Mediaeval Food Tradition

C. ANNE WILSON

Nouvelle cuisine has recently alerted us to the visual aspects of mealtimes because of the decorative and colourful patterns in which prepared foods are laid out upon the plates. But meals have been giving out visual messages since prehistoric times, even though those messages have changed, and have become more or less subtle at different periods.

Some primitive antecedents

We may begin with what Poseidonios says about the Celts living on the fringes of the Roman world early in the first century BC and already receiving the influence of that world through the objects of trade. Several passages have survived from his lost history of the Celts. Two include descriptions of the Celts in Gaul at that time; and one refers to their traditions at a much earlier stage. It is nasty, brutish and short:

> 'And in former times,' he says 'when the hindquarters [of the meat] were served up, the bravest hero took the thigh-piece, and if another man claimed it, they stood up and fought in single combat to the death.'

What this tells us about the appetite and the eye is that in primitive warrior societies the eye is used to assess the choicest articles of food, the appetite is aroused, and then

5

the prize of the finest morsel goes to the strongest eater.

Two other passages by Poseidonios give a rather more domestic picture of the Celts at their meals, and they contain several features which can be regarded as antecedents of the customs practised at mediaeval feasts, in both France and England. He wrote:

> The Celts sit on dried grass, and have their meals served up on wooden tables raised slightly above the earth. Their food consists of a small number of loaves of bread together with a large amount of meat, either boiled, or roasted on charcoal or on spits. They partake of this in a cleanly but leonine fashion, raising up whole limbs in both hands and biting off the meat, while any part which is hard to tear off they cut through with a small dagger which hangs attached to their sword-sheath in its own scabbard. Those who live beside the rivers or near the Mediterranean or Atlantic also eat fish baked with the addition of salt, vinegar and cummin . . . When a large number dine together, they sit around in a circle with the most influential man in the centre, whether he surpasses the others in warlike skill, or nobility of family, or wealth. Beside him sits the host, and next on either side the others, in order of distinction. Their shieldbearers stand behind them, while their spearsmen are seated in a circle on the opposite side and feast in common, like their lords. The servers bear around the drink in earthenware or silver vessels. The trenchers on which they serve the food are also of these materials, others are of bronze, or are wooden or woven baskets. The drink of the wealthy people is wine imported from Italy or the area around Marseilles . . . The lowlier people drink wheaten beer prepared with

honey, though most drink it plain. It is called
corma. They drink from the same cup a little at a
time, not more than a mouthful, but they do it
rather frequently. The boy serves the cup towards
the right, [not] towards the left.[1]

Elsewhere Poseidonios wrote about the Celts in the
more northerly parts of France.

'When dining, they all sit not on chairs, but on
the earth, strewing beneath them the skins of
wolves or dogs. At their meals they are served by
their youngest grown-up children, both boys and
girls. Beside them are hearths blazing with fire,
with cauldrons and spits containing large pieces
of meat. Brave warriors they honour with the
finest portions of the meat.[2]

They were still inclined to resort to duels after the meal,
when they had over-indulged in wine and beer and had
become rumbustious and argumentative. But their feasts
had taken on a certain degree of formality. There were
blazing fires, the meat on the spits and the large
cauldrons, as well as other visual signals: the wooden
tables laid out specially for the meal; the rituals for serving
both food and drink; the silver and bronze plates and
cups. The feasts of the Celts had already become
occasions for tribal leaders to demonstrate conspicuous
wealth to the assembled company. The company itself was
divided up, with the most important people at the centre
of the circle, where everyone could see and recognise
them. So appetites from earliest times were stimulated by
the sense of occasion, and also by the shared feeling of
belonging to the group wherein each person had his
position, whether as a rich, influential man at the centre,
or as a shieldbearer from one of the poorer families. There
are also the beginnings of a sense of theatre in the
arrangement: the appetites of the spectators are whetted
as they watch while the food is served out until they

receive their own share. One other point to notice is that, in this society of warriors, feasts were still very much a male affair. There is no mention of women being present, apart from the teenage girl servers with their brothers. Once the women were married, their place was no longer at the open-air feasts.

Within this tribal scene of communal eating, antecedents can be recognised for several practices customary at feasts in both France and England during the Middle Ages: special rituals for the serving out of the food and drink, the cups and plates of precious or valuable metals, and the prominent position accorded to honoured guests. These were all visual aspects of the meal which continued to be important well over a thousand years after Poseidonios wrote about the Celts in Gaul. The foods of the feast became more sophisticated, of course, and the rituals were infinitely more complex by the time they came to be recorded in detail in the late Middle Ages.

Rituals of the mediaeval feast The outdoor feast did not disappear entirely. Very large communal meals had to be held out of doors; there were some occasions, as for instance when everyone belonging to a big manorial estate, plus many visitors from outside, were present for a special festival, when even the Great Hall was not great enough to hold the multitude. At such times not only were the oxen and other animal foods roasted in the open air, but trestle tables were set up outside as well, and all the other food was carried out.

But the indoor feast was more usual, held in the Hall of the castle or manor-house. There the wooden trestles and boards, and the forms which served as seating for ordinary diners, were laid out along one or both of the long sides of the Hall, while the high table stood on a raised dais at one end. At that table the host and his family and special guests ate their meal. The most important person present (the host, or the principal guest) was seated on a chair beneath a canopy, and was easily identified by everyone in

8

the Hall. The rest of the group at the high table sat on stools, or sometimes two or three of them shared a high-backed settle, facing outwards across the table, with the wall behind them, in a prime position to gaze down the length of the Hall and watch the servants approaching with the food.[3] At the far end, opposite to the dais, was built the carved wooden screen, with its doors onto the screens passage. This passage led from the kitchen and the buttery to the Hall.

Much ceremony attended the serving forth of both food and drink in royal and noble households of the late Middle Ages.[4] Before the company assembled, the high table was laid with no fewer than three cloths – the lowest called the couch, the other two carefully arranged to hang over the edge of the board or table, one at the front and the other at the back. A cloth of sumptuous material was also laid over the cup-board, which was another board set on trestles, placed near the high table. Fifteenth-century illustrations show that a high-backed frame with shelves across it, rather like the back of a Welsh dresser, was at that period fixed behind the flat cup-board. On the shelves were displayed richly decorated silver or silver-gilt cups, bowls and jugs, while on the cup-board itself the special cup for the king or noble lord and the ewer and basin for his personal hand-washing were laid out, with basins and ewers for the hand-washing of other high-table guests at the sides.

A magnificent silver-gilt or silver salt-cellar was set on the high table, to the right of the place of the king or lord; his trenchers of bread were squared and laid out, together with his knife and his spoon resting on a napkin, and the little loaves of bread called manchets, and the whole place-setting was covered with another napkin. The rest of the high table was laid in similar manner, and then the salt-cellars, trencher-bread and cups were set out on the boards in the lower hall for the rest of the company.

When the cooks reported that the meal was ready,

many more rituals were carried out: the covered bread and cutlery were uncovered; the guests and members of the household entered the hall; the *surnappe* (another long cloth) was spread ceremoniously across the high table in front of the principal diners to protect their clothes and the place-settings while they washed their hands in water brought by the ewerer with his ewer and basins. At the meals of the highest nobility, ranking from the king himself down to the earls, *assays* were performed on the salt, the trencher-bread, and even on the water and towels with which the greatest lords and ladies –if any ladies were present –would wash and dry their hands. Assaying meant that various officials of the household (the sewer, the panter, the ewerer and the cupbearer) tested for poison those things that the noblest feasters would touch or eat, by dipping a little triangle of bread into each pottage and sauce and then eating these samples; and by drinking a little of the wine or of the hand-washing water. Even the towel was not exempt; 'Then the Marshall kysseth the towell for his assay, and so layeth it on the left shoulder of the Lorde of the House.'[5]

The hand-washing was not confined to the noble lords; everyone present washed before eating. Water was sometimes brought by the ewerer's assistants – his yeoman and his grooms – for the lowlier guests, but otherwise they washed at a *laving-place* set in the wall of the Hall itself, or in a vestibule very close by. Hand-washing was a necessary prelude to the meal, because all solid food had to be taken up in the fingers in the absence of forks. (The only forks in use in the Middle Ages were the rare examples of the two-pronged version used occasionally in the highest circles to spear the fruits preserved in jars of syrup.) The guests with their washed hands were then conducted to their seats according to their rank and precedence by the marshall; and grace was said.

As the servants came into the Hall bearing the laden

platters and dishes, first to the high table, they passed the lowlier members of the household and guests who caught a glimpse of the foody delights to come: flesh meats and fishes on platters and covered bowls concealing rich pottages. They would also have seen at least one or two extra special and subtle dishes, which were destined for the high table alone.

The Boke of Curtasye offers a useful tip – 'a soteltie I will thee kenne' – to the sewer when he has to carry in a silver bowl filled with boiling pottage; he should put pieces of bread between the dish and his hands: 'Take the brede corvyn [carven] and lay by-twene / And kepe the[e] well hit be not sene.'[6] The carver carved up the roasted and boiled fleshmeat and fishes for the high table, usually working on the open front part of the table, and he set the meat on the slices of trencher-bread. Food for the high-table diners was assayed. The wine-cups were filled in turn, and those for the greatest men were assayed by the cupbearer, who drank a few drops poured into the cover of the cup. Finally, the feasters in the lower hall received their food and wine or ale, and could consume the first course for which the long ceremonial had prepared them.

Meanwhile at the high table the host or hostess offered special titbits to favoured guests. The thirteenth-century rules for the household of the Countess of Lincoln state (in Anglo-Norman French, here translated):

> and order that your dish be so refilled and
> heaped up, especially with the *entremets* [i.e. the
> delicacies] that you may courteously give from
> your dish to right and left to all at your high
> table and to whom else it pleases you, that they
> have the same as you had in front of you.

The editors of *Curye on Inglysch* suggest that this was why a dish called *Checones in critone* in one cookery-book was prepared with a quarter of a chicken each for commoners, but 'a hole checkyn for a lorde'.[7] Some other recipes give similar instructions. The table in the lower hall nearest to the high table on the noble Lord's right-hand side was known as the *reward* because it seated the guests next in importance to those granted places at the high table itself; and individual favourite guests there, too, received titbits from his bowl.

The second course eventually followed, and sometimes even a third course, after which the high table was *voided* with further ceremonies. The *alms* dish, into which portions of food had been piled during the meal, was carried off by the almoner who distributed the contents to the poor at the gate. The *surnappe* was spread out once more over the high table, and grace was said. Then, after further assaying of the washing-water and the towel, the great lord washed again and so did the company at the high table and the guests in the lower hall. Then the tablecloths were removed, and the high table and its chair of estate and its stools and benches, and the trestles and boards and forms of the lower hall were all taken away. Finally, 'the Lorde must drynke wyne standyng, and all other in lyke maner, and that done, every man departeth at his good pleasure.'[8]

This is a very brief account of a great mediaeval feast, which does not do credit to the full tally of rituals performed by the sewer and the carver, the butler and the cupbearer, the panter and the ewerer. But it is enough to show how tedious such occasions were. Yet the meal was enlivened by the amount of spectacle the company in the main body of the Hall could observe, while they all waited their turn to receive their own tepid food. They could watch the comings and goings of the various household officers in their fine livery, and could feast their eyes upon the rich garments of the principal guests and the display of silver and gilded vessels at the cup-board. And they could admire the appearance of the food itself, as it came into sight. Minstrels were present at all the most important feasts, so that there was entertainment for the ears as well as the eyes, with singing to the harp and to other instruments.

The smaller feasts held in the Great Halls of manor houses up and down the country were much simpler. But even there the retainers, seated at the boards in the lower hall, would have often had to wait and watch as the food was carried first to the high table, to be served out to the lord and his lady and their special guests.

The food itself came in many forms. There were pottages, **Food as spectacle** both the runny ones containing gobbets of meat, roots and herbs, which were poured over a sop of toasted bread at the bottom of the bowl, and the very thick ones, described as 'standing' and of the consistency of today's porridge, or even thicker. There were the boiled fleshmeats and fishes, and the roast meats and fowls, and the special sauces served with them. There were bakemeats, which included meat pasties; pies containing shredded meat, fish or eggs with dried fruits; and various types of custard baked in pastry shells or *coffins*. There were fritters, pancakes and other fried delicacies. And there were *leaches*, solid confections based, often, on milk-curds or breadcrumbs moistened with honey, which were stiff enough to be cut and eaten in slices.

Many of these foods were deliberately prepared so as to have strong visual interest. The pottages were *flourished,* or decorated with a scattering of spice-powder and sugar over the surface, or occasionally with yolks of hard-boiled eggs. A meat jelly was planted with laurel leaves; and a tart with an egg and pork filling was planted, more substantially, with small birds and pieces of rabbit.[9] White pottages were garnished with red aniseed comfits, and red or dark ones with white sugar comfits. The *flampeyn,* a pastry tart, had points or triangles of pastry standing upright in its filling.[10] At the grandest feasts of all, bands of gold or silver foil were laid over very rich, thick pottages, or used to decorate fillets of boar. A whole sucking-pig decorated with a bar of gold and a bar of silver could be served to a very great lord.[11]

The boar's head, carried in for the first course, was sent from the kitchen 'with the snout well-garlanded'. The small meat-animals, such as sucking-pigs and coneys, and all the fishes that came whole to the table, were brought in looking lifelike with their heads still on. The same was true of some of the birds, including cranes, herons and curlews. A peacock would have had its neck broken in the kitchen, and its skin and feathers, with the head, carefully removed. The body was roasted sitting on the spit 'as he was wonte to sitte alyve'. When done, it was removed from the spit and cooled. 'And then', says the recipe, 'wynde the skyn with the fethurs and taile about the body, and serve him forth as he were a-live.'[12] For good measure, his comb and his beak could be gilded with gold leaf. This would have been described by the feasters as a 'soteltie'.

Sotelties are defined in *Curye on Inglysch* as 'foods made to look like something else, e.g. birds covered with their feathers to look 'alive', and sugar sculptures of human figures, etc.'[13] The sugar sculptures are frequently encountered on mediaeval menus for great feasts, where the last item on the list of dishes for each of the two or three courses is 'a soteltie'.

Those very specialised sotelties were some of the most spectacular confections to be carried through the Hall during a feast. The simplest ones comprised a single figure for each course, such as those which appeared at the enthronement feast of the Bishop of Salisbury in 1417: the soteltie at the end of the first course was a figure of the Lamb of God: at the end of the second course, a leopard; at the end of the third course, an eagle.[14]

As the Middle Ages drew to a close, some of the sotelties had become very complex indeed, and they tended to be modelled in plaster and wood rather than in marzipan. The sotelties produced for the enthronization feast of the Archbishop of Canterbury in 1504 were probably of this kind, so extensive that they had to be carried in on three separate boards. Those following the second course were: first, a scene in which the Archbishop received his pall in the presence of the Pope, the cardinals and other bishops; second, a reproduction of the enthronization scene itself; while the third board contained 'a church and a choir with singing men in surplices, and doctors in their grey *amises* [hoods] at a desk with a book written and noted with the Office of the Mass born up and well garnished with angels'.[15]

Sotelties of the other kind, that is items of food made to look like something else, gave the cook a chance to display his ingenuity; and several recipes were recorded in cookery-book manuscripts. A capon was carefully skinned, like the peacock, and its body was roasted and basted with a batter of almond milk and fine flour. Meanwhile, the skin was filled up with a forcemeat of hen's flesh, egg yolks and spices, and was also roasted and basted with egg yolks. Then the body and stuffed skin were served up side by side. This confection was adapted from Arab cookery, as four recipes for the stuffing of the empty skin of a fowl are listed in M. Rodinson's summary of the contents of the thirteenth-century Arabic cookery-book, *Kitab al-Wusla ila l'habib*. The beef or mutton *allowes* of mediaeval cookery were originally 'larks' (Old French *aloes*) which means that they were viewed as imitation birds. To make them, steaks cut from beef or mutton were rolled up around a forcemeat of herbs, egg yolks and suet or beef-marrow, and were roasted on a spit. A fifteenth-century recipe adds: 'If thou wilt, thou may endore them [i.e. baste them with a golden batter of egg yolks and saffron] and make them a service.'[16]

A fantastic animal called a *cockagrys* was made by cutting off the legs of a cock and sewing its body to the hindquarters of a young pig (also called a *gris*), filling the combined interior with forcemeat. It was parboiled, then roasted on a spit, and basted with egg-yolks and saffron; and finally it was decorated with gold and silver leaf, and served forth in all its glory.[17]

Urchins, or hedgehogs, were created from the maws (stomach-bags) of pigs and were stuffed with forcemeat (in a recipe in the *Forme of Cury*, one great swine's maw surrounded by six little pig's maws); these were pricked all over with split almonds, or sometimes with quills of fried pastry. They were roasted on a spit, and basted with a batter coloured yellow with saffron, green with shredded parsley or black with blood.[18] A special thick pottage of pears was served with a lion rampant made of yellow-coloured pastry standing in each bowl.[19] For a confection called *pottewys*, forcemeat was stuffed into flowerpot moulds or actual pots, which were broken open once they had been given a good boiling; then the shaped stuffings were roasted on a spit, and were basted with yellow or green batter; and when they were taken off, pastry roses coloured red or white were arranged with their stalks in the central hole where the spit had been. This last recipe was evidently borrowed from Spanish Arab cookery, for it is also found in one of the versions of the French *Viandier* under the title 'pots of Spain'.[20]

The colours of food and their significance A very important element in most of the pottages and sauces, as well as in the more elaborate confections, was that of colour. At our meals today, we identify the main ingredients of our food by their colours, and if they are either duller or muddier than we expect, or seem too glaring and artificial-looking, then our appetite for the food itself is diminished. So close is the link between vision and the sense of taste that modern food manufacturers have found that if they can get the colour of a processed food, such as a fruit mousse or fruit cream, just right – that is, if the colour is precisely what the consumer expects it to be – then it is possible to add less of the real flavour of the fruit. The eye actually supplies some part of what is needed to create the sensation of the full, rich taste for the eater.[21]

The fact that colour can enhance the appeal of foodstuffs was recognised in Roman times. For instance, a preference for meat dishes with rich, dark gravy led Roman cooks to add *defrutum* to their more pallid stews *'ut coloret'*–to give them a deeper colour. *Defrutum* was wine boiled down to concentrate its flavour, colour and sweetness, and kept in store as a condiment.[22] As an alternative, they added wine itself. Apicius revealed another cookery secret since beloved of institutional cooks: 'All green vegetables become bright emerald green if boiled with cooking soda.'[23] He also gave recipes for three sauces called 'white sauce' from their ingredients, comprising such items as hard-boiled egg-whites, pine kernels, white pepper, white wine, onion rings; and one called 'green sauce', made with green herbs.[24] In all these examples, the visual appeal was in the natural colours of the foodstuffs, or at least in an enhanced version of the natural colour. It is interesting that saffron was *not* employed to highlight the colour of yellow dishes; but it *was* added to spiced wine and to absinthe, thus introducing a strong artificial colour into those wines.

Only in the later Middle Ages, however, were saffron and other bright plant dyes taken into European cookery on a large scale, to create effects which often bore little relationship to the original colours of the main ingredients from which a dish was composed. The catalyst in this was, of course, Arab cuisine, adopted from the Saracens and adapted to western tastes in the Crusader states at the eastern end of the Mediterranean; and from there it reached the Franks and Normans of western Europe. The Normans also had experience of Arab cookery in Sicily. Finally, the partly-Arabic cuisine of southern Spain began to exert some influence on north-western Europe.

Arab cookery was inherited from the Persian empire

which flourished between the third and seventh centuries AD, and sadly we have no recipe book from that era. But we do have English translations of two mediaeval Arab documents about food. One is a series of poems of the tenth century AD in praise of several favourite confections of Arab cookery. The other is part of a cookery book translated from a manuscript of the year 1226, and called by the translator, *A Baghdad Cookery Book*.[25] In both there are many golden, saffron-tinted dishes, and also some red ones, and the poems refer several times to white and scarlet, gold and silver, and vermilion. The delight of the mediaeval Arabs in these food colours had its origins not in their food experience, but in medicine and in alchemy.

Gold itself, on account of its longevity, was regarded by Arab physicians as a medicine which would lengthen the span of human life. Those who could not afford to consume real gold could at least consume its colour in saffron-tinted food, and could thus ingest some tiny part of the life-enhancing quality of gold. Red and white, the other two favourite colours of Arab cookery, were connected with cinnabar, that is, mercury sulphide, and with mercury itself. Cinnabar, which is the red earth known as vermilion, was the starting material for the alchemist, who extracted mercury from cinnabar, and then tried with the help of sulphur to turn it into gold. Red food shared the colour of cinnabar, and white food came close to the silver colour of mercury, and both were beneficial to the eater because their colours were those of gold while it was still passing through its uncompleted stages.

In China, the Taoist alchemists used to eat small quantities of cinnabar and other minerals, on a regular basis, in their attempt to achieve immortality. In fact, they died prematurely as a result; but the chemicals trapped in their bodies preserved them for some time, thus giving the impression that the alchemists had at least been on the way to becoming immortal. Something of this idea had clearly travelled along the trade routes to the Arabs in Persia and Syria. Two recipes in the *Baghdad Cookery Book*, one for a form of halva, the other for a savoury relish, include vermilion as a red food dye, which cannot have done much good to those who ate it. A related Chinese idea which also reached the Arabs was that the next best thing to consuming actual gold was to eat other food off yellow and red plates. In one of the tenth-century Arabic food poems, the foods of the feast are indeed served in red and yellow bowls.[26]

It was this golden food which made the greatest impact on the Crusaders when they experienced Saracen cuisine during more than two hundred years in Jerusalem, Antioch and the other Crusader kingdoms at the eastern end of the Mediterranean. Those who returned to Europe soon made sure that saffron was adopted into both French and English cookery. Saffron crocuses were cultivated in Spain, and from there saffron was imported into England; though eventually a certain amount was also grown in England, in Essex and Cambridgeshire. Saffron appears frequently in the *gauncils* and the *civies*, the *bukkenades* and the *gravies*, the *jussels* and the *bruets*, of the mediaeval cookery-books of France and England, and many a yellow pottage and sauce must have been carried through the Hall on a feast day.

In the *Ménagier de Paris*, the French household book written about 1393, a distinction is made between the use of saffron, well ground in the mortar, mixed with ground breadcrumbs and strained with broth, then amalgamated with the liquid base of a stew or sauce, and the decorative sprinkling of the saffron over the top, which created little areas of gold on the surface: 'for that which is strained is to give colour, that which is sprinkled on the top is said to be *fringed (frangé)*.'[27] Although there is no English equivalent for this cookery term, this same use for saffron can be recognised here and there, as in a recipe for boiled partridge: 'and when the partridge is boiled enough, take the pot off the fire, and when thou shalt serve him forth, cast into the pot powder-ginger, salt, saffron, and serve forth'.[28] Again, in the recipe for a thick white pottage which ends, 'Take a vessel y-holed and put in saffron', it was evidently meant to be shaken above the surface of the pottage, which was served in forthwith.[29]

Among the thick pottages, saffroned rice was most obviously borrowed from Saracen cookery.[30] By association of ideas, the northern wheat-based pottage called *frumenty* was also coloured with saffron: it was served along with venison on a meat-day and with porpoise on a fish-day. 'Grewel enforced' was the name of another thick pottage, made from oatmeal with ground-up pork, and this was saffroned too. An influence from another area of Saracen cookery, also recorded in the *Baghdad Cookery Book*, was the use of saffron in the forcemeat of breadcrumbs, eggs and spices that stuffed a sheep's maw to make a mediaeval haggis-pudding. Such puddings were still being given the saffron colouring at the end of Queen Elizabeth's reign.[31]

Minced-meat balls glazed with yolk of egg were called, in menu French, *pommes d'orange* or *pommes dorrées;* and they came to the West straight from Arab cookery. They are named *naranjiya* (the Arab word for oranges) in the *Baghdad Cookery Book*. They were made of ground-up meat (mutton or chicken for the Saracens; pork or beef for French and Anglo-Norman cooks). The Arabic recipe included real bitter-orange juice, as well as saffron, to colour the meat mixture. The French and Anglo-Norman cooks had to make do with saffron only! At the time when this recipe first reached them, real oranges were still too rare in northern Europe for their juice to be a regular cookery ingredient. The meatballs were roasted on spits and basted with a batter of egg-yolks and saffron as they cooked. If shredded parsley was added to the

batter instead of saffron, they could be made into green
pommes or 'apples'.[32]

The saffron-coloured foods were welcomed into
French cuisine as readily as into English. But when it came
to other colours, the cookery of the Franks lagged behind
that of the Anglo-Normans. The earliest manuscript of
the *Viandier* goes nowhere beyond the yellow of saffron
and the green of shredded parsley. Yet there are some
very distinctive coloured confections in the fourteenth-
century English recipe book called *Diversa Cibaria*. Here
we find the use of both red fruits and of a red colouring-
herb called *sangdragon*; and of red wine and powdered
cloves to produce indigo. Moreover, a still earlier Norman
French version of the first 32 recipes exists, and has now
been published.[33] This takes the collection back yet
further, to the period when the Anglo-Norman nobility
and their households in England still spoke French.

All 32 recipes are very colour-oriented indeed: 12 are red,
8 yellow, 7 white, 3 green, 1 indigo and 1 mutli-coloured; 25
of them actually state in the recipe that 'the colour shall be
red' (or 'yellow', or whichever colour it was), thus
indicating that they had been selected specifically for
their colours. One (no. 4) is called 'Food of Spain'
(*Viaunde.despyne*) and, like many others, it is based upon a
mixture of rice-flour and chicken meat moistened with
almond milk, but it is coloured yellow, flavoured with
cloves, and scattered with pistachio nuts. These nuts
appear twice more in this small recipe collection, and
nowhere else in English mediaeval cookery-books. And
the multi-coloured dish has the title 'Turk's head' and is
just that: a filled open tart, with a thick top layer of nut
paste in red, yellow and green, showing the features of a
man's face, while the container is a black bowl to
represent his hair.

What we have here is a recipe-book very closely
connected with Saracen cookery, which, if not translating
actual Arabic recipes, has at least produced close

adaptations of them suited to English ingredients. It could have originated in Sicily, or even in Antioch as the great Norman families of Normandy and England maintained close links with their kinsfolk who settled in South Italy and Sicily, and in the eastern Kingdom of Antioch.[34] From the 32 Norman-French recipes subsequently translated into English, we can see that what had struck the Normans above all else about Saracen cookery was the brightly coloured dishes. The recipes were compiled for people who were truly fascinated by the white blancmanges, the red stews and sauces, and the golden saffroned confections of Saracen cookery.

White or coloured versions of the Saracen pounded chicken, rice and sugar mixture (the progenitor of the 'blancmange' of French and English mediaeval cookery-books) are the basis for many of the recipes in this colourful Anglo-Norman compilation. This is the case for the first three recipes called respectively *Blanc desire* (i.e. *Blanc de Syrie*=white food of Syria), *Vert desire* (green food of Syria) and *Jaune desire* (yellow food of Syria, actually written *Ane [d]esire* in the manuscript). In all of them the rice takes the form of rice-flour, and the solid ingredients are mixed with almond milk and spices. The white dish is to be made in 'a place without filth', the green one is coloured with parsley, and the yellow one with saffron. Recipe no. 7 is the indigo-coloured *mawmeny*, another name well known in the mediaeval cookery-books of western Europe, and deriving probably from Arabic *ma'muniya*, a sweetened chicken and rice confection.[35] Here the recipe contains not only pounded capon-flesh (boiled in red wine and further darkened with powdered cloves) with sugar and ground almonds, but also ground-up 'great flesh', a term which translated the French *grosse char* and denotes the fleshmeat of the larger beasts, either pork, mutton or beef.

Four more sweet, thick pottages are given (nos. 11–14) in which the fleshmeat element is supplied only by 'great flesh'. There is no mention of pounding or grinding, but since the 'great flesh' is listed in the middle of the ingredients, in three cases before the spices and sugar, it was obviously part of the main recipe (with the pounding necessary to produce the proper consistency understood), not a separate meat item for which the recipe supplies a sauce. The pottages are all thickened with rice-flour or *amidon* (very fine wheat-flour). *Spinette* is flavoured with plenty of hawthorn blossoms, *Rosee* with rose-petals, *Freyses* with strawberries, and *Scirresez* with cherries. Each is finally garnished with a scattering of the appropriate flower-petals or fruits on the surface.

The *Baghdad Cookery Book* has a red stew of mutton with redcurrant juice; and a thick confection of shredded chicken cooked with pounded pistachios and sugar.[36] The English translation of this book is much abridged, and there may be other recipes still closer to the Anglo-Norman ones in the complete Arabic text. Rodinson gives a tantalising list of recipe titles for chicken cooked with rose conserve; with mulberry conserve; with dates; with quinces; with prunes; and with other fruits including, possibly, wild cherries.[37] But the *Wusla* has not been published yet in any western language translation, so again we cannot make direct comparisons with recipes in mediaeval English cookery-books. The Saracen influences are clear, but there is also a degree of adaptation by Anglo-Norman cooks.

One of the white recipes in the group of colour-coded recipes in *Diversa Cibaria* (no. 23) is for a meatless white pottage of elderflowers composed only of the crushed flowers, amidon, almond milk and 'ginger great plenty'; it is of course strewn with elder blossoms before being served. But a version made with chicken (or turbot on a fish day) appears in the next group of recipes in *Diversa Cibaria* (as no. 44). These are English translations of some recipes in another Norman French collection, which exists in a late thirteenth-century manuscript now also published.[38] The instructions for the elderflower pottage conclude with advice to gather the flowers in season, let them dry, then grind them in a mortar to keep all through the year.

In both the Norman French manuscript and *Diversa Cibaria* (nos. 35–37) there are further recipes for hawthorn, rose and strawberry pottages; and these too have already lost their meat and are to be made with almond milk or cow's milk, and thickened with eggs and breadcrumbs. Sugar is sprinkled over the rose pottage, but otherwise they are unsweetened.[39] Lack of meat represents a significant development from the Saracen blancmange-type pottage at the hands of the Anglo-Norman cooks. Most of the fourteenth- and fifteenth-century recipes for strawberry, cherry and flower-petal pottages are meatless. The recipe for *rosee* in the *Forme of Cury* says: 'Cast thereto sugar, a good portion', and it adds spices, pinenuts and dates as well.[40] Primrose and violet pottages were created, flower pottages for even earlier in the year than the hawthorn version.[41] There are further sweet pottages coloured by dye-plants, purple ones made with turnsole, and a red confection called 'Saracen's blood' (*Saunc Sarazine*), reddened with alkenet root or with crushed rosehips.[42] From these gaily coloured thick pottages, in which cow's milk often replaced the earlier almond milk, the English developed their taste for sweet, solid milk puddings, which have never been a great part of the French food tradition.

The prime importance of colour is attested by the pottage named *murree* made with mulberries and veal or chicken. Two or three mulberry versions were copied into fourteenth- and fifteenth-century cookery-books.[43] Yet in the *murree* in the late thirteenth-century Norman French collection of highly coloured recipes, the actual berries have already been replaced with the food dye, red sandalwood. This second type of *murree* also reappeared in the later mediaeval recipe books;[44] it had the advantage of being available at all times of year. But its treatment suggests that the colour of a *murree* was more important than the flavour of the mulberries from which the pottage took its name. Colour often seems to have been valued more for its own sake in English mediaeval cookery than as a signal of the ingredients of the dish. This was certainly true of jellies set from meat or fish stock: they were saffron-coloured at first, but later also tinted purple with turnsole or indigo, and red with alkenet or sanders (red sandalwood).[45] The only variation in flavour was that supplied by the various colouring agents.

The thick coloured pottages were often *departed* with a pottage of another colour: a portion of each of two colours was laid in every bowl, and served forth. A white blancmange or similar white confection was departed with a contrasting shade, with the green *Vert desire*, for instance, or with the red *Sandale* of ground-up chicken-meat and pork, coloured with red sandalwood. Or half of a pottage was left white, and the other half yellowed with saffron.[46] The primrose pottage was accentuated with saffron, and then was departed with the violet one. A jelly of one colour was left to set in a ring of pastry in the middle of a large dish; when it was cold and solid, the pastry was removed and the space round the edge filled up with jelly of a second colour.[47]

Another favourite area for colour effects was tart-fillings: red tarts were not the jam tarts that we know, but tarts containing a chicken and rice-flour filling tinted, once again, with sanders or alkanet. *Dowsets* were tarts filled with saffroned custard. More elaborate tarts were divided into four, with each section filled separately with white, yellow and green mixtures; the fourth section, described as 'black' sometimes contained a composition of pounded figs, raisins and dates, and sometimes one made with animal blood, like a black pudding. Pastry itself was often coloured yellow with saffron.

At the mediaeval feast, these coloured foodstuffs

evidently appealed to the eye nearly as much as the more elaborate sotelties, to judge by their frequent appearance in recipe-books and in menus. The pride of the cook in producing a visually interesting dish is reflected in the final instruction of a fourteenth-century recipe for stuffed cherries piled up in a silver bowl: 'Beor the mes to the deys tovoren alle men' (Bear the mess to the dais before everyone).[48]

Notes and References

1. Athenaeus, IV, 40. 154A–C; and IV.36.151E–152D.
2. Diodorus Siculus, V.28.4.
3. The furnishings of the Hall are discussed more fully below in *From Mediaeval Castle Hall to Eighteenth-century Country-house Dining-room*, p.28.
4. The information in the following section is drawn from R. Warner, *Antiquitates Culinariae* (London, 1795), pp. 99–105; J. Russell, *The Boke of Nurture;* and *The Boke of Curtasaye*; both ed. F. J. Furnival (Early English Text Society, OS 32, 1868).
5. Warner, p. 101.
6. *Boke of Curtasaye*, p. 202.
7. Thirteenth-century household rules for the Countess of Lincoln, quoted in C. B. Hieatt & S. Butler, eds, *Curye on Inglysch* (Early English Text Society, SS 8, 1985), p. 6; Warner, p. 80.
8. Warner, p. 105.
9. Hieatt & Butler, *Curye on Inglysch* (hereafter *C. on I.*), II, no. 56; *Forme of Cury* (= *C. on I.*, IV) no. 176.
10. *Forme of Cury*, nos. 116; 192.
11. Warner, pp. 76; 79; 80.
12. Walter of Bibbesworth, in *C. on I.*, p. 3; T. Austin, ed. *Two Fifteenth-century Cookery-Books* (Early English Text Society, OS 91, 1888), p. 79.
13. *C. on I.*, p. 215 s.v. 'sotilteis'.
14. Austin, pp. 69–70.
15. Warner, p. 114.
16. *C. on I.*, II, no. 28; M. Rodinson, 'Recherches sur les documents arabes relatives à la cuisine', *Revue des Etudes Islamiques* 17 (1949), p. 133; C. B. Hieatt, ed., *An Ordinance of Pottage (MS Yale Beinecke 163)*, (London, 1988), p. 61.
17. *Forme of Cury*, no. 183; Austin, p. 115.
18. *Forme of Cury*, no. 184; Austin, p. 38.
19. *C. on I.*, I, no. 24.
20. *Forme of Cury* no. 185; *C. on I*, p. 208, s.v. 'Potte wys'.
21. Information supplied by a chemist in the food-processing sector.
22. Apicius, *The Roman Cookery-Book*, ed. B. Flower & E. Rosenbaum (London, 1958), VI.2.1 and 3.
23. Ibid., III.1.

24. Ibid., V.3.2.; VI.5.3 and 5.
25. A. J. Arberry, 'A Baghdad Cookery Book', *Islamic Culture* 13 (1939), pp. 21–47; 189–214. The introduction includes a selection of the poems.
26. Ibid., pp. 208; 210; 21. See also C. A. Wilson 'The Saracen connection, part 1', *Petits Propos Culinaires* 7 (1981), pp. 16–18.
27. *Ménagier de Paris*, ed. G. E. Brereton & J. M. Ferrier (Oxford, 1981), p. 218; *Goodman of Paris* = abridged ed., English translation by E. Power (London, 1928), p. 265.
28. Austin, p. 9.
29. *Forme of Cury*, no. 39.
30. Arberry, pp. 44; 46; *Forme of Cury*, no. 11.
31. Arberry, p. 199; *C. on I.*, II, no. 15; Austin, p. 39; C. A. Wilson, 'A Cookery-book and its Context: Elizabethan Cookery and Lady Fettiplace', *Petits Propos Culinaires* 25 (1987), p. 20.
32. Arberry, p. 190; P. Aebischer, 'Un manuscrit Valaisan du *Viandier* attribué à Taillevent, *Vallesia* 8 (1953), p. 92; C. B. Hieatt & R. F. Jones, 'Two Anglo-Norman culinary collections', *Speculum* 61 (1986), p. 862; *Forme of Cury*, no. 182, etc.
33. *C. on I.*, I, nos. 1–32; Hieatt & Jones, 'Two Anglo-Norman culinary collections', pp. 866–8.
34. D. C. Douglas, *The Norman Achievement* (London, 1972, Fontana), pp. 110–28.
35. *C. on I.*, 200 s.v. *maumenee*; Rodinson, p. 139.
36. Arberry, pp. 38; 197.
37. Rodinson, pp. 133–4.
38. Hieatt & Jones, pp. 862-6.
39. Ibid., p. 864.
40. *Forme of Cury*, no. 53.
41. *C. on I.*, nos. 34 and 35; Austin, pp. 25; 29.
42. *C. on I.*, III, no. 16; *Forme of Cury*, no. 86; Austin, pp. 30; 113.
43. *C. on I.*, II, no. 47; Austin, p. 28 (two versions of the same recipe).
44. *C. on I.*, I, no. 32: *Forme of Cury*, no. 40; Austin, p. 19.
45. *C. on I.*, I, no. 25; II, no. 36; Austin, 87; Warner, p. 61.
46. *C. on I.*, I, no. 29; II, no. 34; Austin, p. 20.
47. Warner, p. 61.
48. *C. on I.*, I, no. 54.

3.

From Mediaeval Great Hall to Country-house Dining-room: The Furniture and Setting of the Social Meal

C. ANNE WILSON

About 1425 a scribe made a copy of the *Form of Cury*, the great cookery-book produced at the English court some thirty-five years earlier. As a preface to this copy he wrote:

'The *Forme of Cury* was compiled by the chief Master Cooks of King Richard the Second, King of England after the Conquest, the which was accounted the best and royalest viandier of all Christian kings.'[1]

Those words 'best and royalest' do not refer to the size of the king's appetite, or even simply to the quality and quantity of the food of his household. The giving of a great feast in mediaeval times involved much more than just a large and interesting menu.

Feasts were, above all, occasions for display. The appearance of the food was at least as important as its flavour; and the appearance of the surroundings within which it was served was perhaps the most important feature of all. The setting of the feast was an expression of the status of the host and of the principal guests, often referred to in mediaeval documents as their 'estate'. Precedence played a vital role in courtly and noble social life; and the rituals of table-laying, of serving forth the two or three courses of the feast, and of concluding the meal and clearing away the remnants, were all designed to emphasise the hierarchical structure of mediaeval society.

Our information about the ways in which these

ceremonies were carried out comes from the ordinances of royal and noble families, and from treatises on etiquette directed to the stewards, butlers, sewers, and other household officials who were responsible for the smooth running of the mealtime arrangements of great and important families. These rituals were echoed on a simpler scale in the manor houses of the knights and other lesser landlords up and down the country.

The background for the visual display was supplied by the Great Hall itself, the largest room of the mediaeval castle or manor house. At non-feasting times it could be a place of assembly for soldiers or peasant workers, and it was also the room where business was conducted between a lord and his tenants. It also served as a thoroughfare for people passing to the inner chambers of the castle. Since it was neither locked up nor watched over during much of the day, it was clearly not a place in which portable articles of value could be left lying about. Most of the furniture associated with dining or feasting was not, therefore, kept permanently in position; and the Hall was dressed afresh for each great feast, like the stage of a theatre at the beginning of a new act.

The Great Hall and its furnishings

Tapestries, silk hangings or cloth-of-gold were unrolled and hung to decorate the walls. Mediaeval lords lived a peripatetic life, moving from one castle to another every few weeks or months. Their valuable hangings and more important pieces of furniture travelled with them, and were brought out to adorn the Hall whenever a grand feast took place.

The ordinary furniture for the Hall was stored near by, sometimes even in the corners of the Hall itself.[2] It comprised the trestles and boards which made up mediaeval tables, and the forms on which lowlier members of the household and the less significant visitors sat to eat their meals; these items were placed at the sides of the Hall and assembled in their proper positions.

The trestle table for the lord and his guests was set across the end of the Hall furthest from the screens passage and the entrance doorways through which the food was carried from the kitchen. From the thirteenth century onwards it was usually raised on a low dais, thus making it the most visible table in the Hall. Behind it were the principal feasters seated in a row and facing down the Hall. When the high table party was a large one, its lesser members sometimes took their places at the two short ends of the table, where they sat on stools. But the long front side of the board was left open, so that the sewer and his assistants could deliver the dishes of food onto the table, and the cupbearer could offer the cups of wine. In the last mediaeval centuries the table on the dais was often kept permanently in position, and was known as a 'table dormant' or simply as a 'dormant': the sheer weight of the board made it unlikely that it would disappear when the Hall was left empty.[3]

The seating arrangements for the feasters at the high table had specific visual messages to offer. The most important person present sat on a chair placed centrally behind the high table. Often he was the host; but the exact observance of the rules of precedence meant that this significant place might be occupied by a guest of higher estate than the host, who then had to sit further down the table. There was usually only one chair on the dais, so the estate of its occupant was immediately recognisable (the tradition survives in the single Chairman of a Board, and the single occupant of the 'chair' of a university department). The other diners at the high table sat either on high-backed benches which seated two or three people side by side, or on stools or forms.

Very great personages had their own chairs of estate which were carried in their baggage when they moved about the country. Sometimes the wood of the chair was painted (in the case of kings, with royal symbols), or decorated with knobs and panels of copper. If it lacked other adornments, it was at least covered with a piece of rich cloth. A chair of estate belonging to the Duchess of Suffolk is described in an inventory of 1446 as being covered with blue cloth-of-gold and panels of copper, and it had 'a case of leather thereto' to protect it when it was carried about.[4]

The estate of the person who sat in the chair was further demonstrated by the *tester*, a decorative piece of cloth hung against the wall directly above the back of the chair, behind the head of the person sitting in it. In the later Middle Ages a canopy was added to project from the wall above the tester over the head of the person in the chair. The canopy was sometimes of wood; but many were of rich cloth, and such a canopy was called a *cloth of estate*.[5] When several very grand personages were present, the tester and canopy or cloth of estate might extend behind and above a group of people seated behind the central part of the table.

The cup-board, placed near the high table, was draped with silk or coloured cloth-of-gold, and the tiers of shelves or stages behind it carried a display of cups and bowls of precious metal finely engraved and sometimes set with jewels. This too was a powerful symbol of the wealth and importance of its owner. In France the cup-board was known as the *buffet* or *dressoir*; and in French court circles of the fifteenth century there was even a code of honour whereby the estate of the cup-board's owner was indicated by the number of tiers that rose behind the board. Alienor de Poitiers, who clearly regarded herself as an expert on matters of estate and precedent, recorded that the wife of a knight of the lowest order had one tier to her cup-board, the wife of a knight banneret had two, a countess had three, a princess had four and the queen had five. But people who sought to create an impression were quite prepared to add a tier or two to their cup-boards; and Alienor noted with disapproval that Marie of Burgundy, daughter of Isabelle of Bourbon and Charles, heir to the

Duke of Burgundy, had five stages to her cup-board or *buffet*, thus vaunting her estate even beyond its original high degree.[6] Like the principal chair at the high table, the cup-boards or *buffets* of the nobility were given canopies, either of wood or of rich textiles, to emphasise their grandeur and make them still more obviously visible to those who dined in the main body of the Hall.

The deployment of sumptuous, highly coloured cloth to drape and conceal the surfaces of the cup-board and its tiers, the high-backed benches on the dais and sometimes even the chair itself, was due in part to the nature of mediaeval furniture. Most pieces were heavy and plain, in England usually of oak. It was only very late in the Middle Ages that carved wood panelling and furniture carved to imitate panelling began to be widely produced, following the invention of the sawmill early in the fourteenth century. Finely carved furniture and wall decorations of wood were signs of conspicuous expenditure in later country houses and had their counterpart within the mediaeval castle or manor house in the display of vividly coloured hangings and draperies.

So, above all, the great feast was a pageant of colour and brightness – the brilliance of the hangings and covering cloths, the glow of gold and silver vessels, the varied hues of the clothes of the principal diners and the heraldic colours of the livery of the many servers who carried their food and drink through the Hall to the dais. In the radiance of the scene must lie an important clue as to why mediaeval festal food was itself so often highly coloured with food-dyes, white, red, purple and, above all, yellow. The saffroned dishes were not there simply to prove that the great lord could afford to flavour his food with expensive spices, nor even because of the possible medicinal significance of the colour yellow.[7] The food had to compete with its background; and the cooked dishes, had they been left in the natural colours of the basic materials after they had been through the cooking process, would have looked altogether too dull and insipid to awaken the appetite in such a setting.

A further stimulus to the appetite was the significance of the occasion, and the emotions it aroused. The gentlemen and lowlier members of the household took pride in the ability of their lord to put on a splendid show: the generous display of possessions was matched by a generous abundance of food, served out to everyone present on a lavish scale. Many of the dishes that were carried to the dais were duplicated by those placed on the board for all the humbler diners in the lower hall (even if a few extra special ones appeared uniquely on the high table). There was the admiration of the principal guests and their entourages, and their pleasure at receiving handsome treatment from a host who was so patently a person of high estate. As Bridget Henisch wrote, in *Fast and Feast*, 'a ceremonial dinner was a visible demonstration of the ties of power, dependence and mutual obligation which bound the host and guests. It was politic for the host to appear generous, because the lavishness of his table gave a clue to his resources .... Just as the host needed his guests, so they needed his invitation.'[8]

Those present at the feast were predominantly male: the only women taking part might be the wife of the host, the wife of the principal guest, and their attendant ladies. The other members of the household who shared in the feast and all the visitors of lowlier rank were men, and they did not bring their wives with them. Social organisation still preserved close links with military organisation. The same was true even at minor feasts and at everyday mealtimes, where the 'strangers' who joined the household for the meal might be messengers or workpeople from outside the lord's immediate domain. Often the lord's wife and her ladies preferred to eat in the Chamber and not to join the diners in the Hall; or the lady chose to make a late and brief appearance only at the high table.

The Great Chamber in the Middle Ages The time came when the lord himself ceased to attend the meal in the Hall. This fashion may have spread downwards from court circles, for it is mentioned in the household regulations of King Edward II and King Edward IV.[9] But it reached as far as the local lord of the manor, for Piers Plowman, in a version of Langland's poem current at the end of the fourteenth century, complained:

> Elynge [wretched] is the hall each day in the week,
> There the Lord nor the Lady liketh not to sit.
> Now hath each rich [person] a rule to eat by
>   himself
> In a privy parlour ...
> Or in a chamber with a chimney, and leave the
>   chief hall
> That was made for meals, for men to eat in,
> And all to spare to spill that spend shall another.[10]

Economy may well have entered into it: if the lord and lady and their immediate guests of like estate enjoyed a sumptuous meal privately in the Chamber, it was no longer necessary for them to supply outstandingly good fare for the large number of lesser folk who ate in the lower hall. The 'chamber with a chimney' gives another clue. The central hearths in Halls throughout the land were gradually replaced by one or more wall-fireplaces over a period that stretched from the twelfth to the fifteenth century. Once a wall-chimney had been installed, an upper room formerly heated by smoky braziers could have the advantage of a fireplace with a fire in it.

So the lord and lady took their meals in the Great Chamber, which was also the lord's bedchamber. It contained his bed with its canopy and hangings, as well as a cup-board bearing a display of silverware; a great chair

1.
Dining in 'a chamber with a chimney'. Note the high-backed chair of the principal diner, with tester and canopy above. ('February' from an early sixteenth century Flemish calendar, British Library MS Add. 24098, fol. 19v.).

with arms for the lord and a smaller one for his lady, and perhaps one or two additional chairs for principal guests; several stools for lesser guests and other members of the host's family; and a trestle table which had to be set up anew each time a meal was served in the Chamber. But since that room was a place of greater security than the

Hall, its furniture could be kept permanently within it behind a locked door, at least during the time when the family was in residence.

When the greatest feasts took place, those that were held to celebrate weddings, christenings and other events calling for large-scale hospitality, the lord and lady returned to the Hall and sat once more at the high table alongside their chief guests. At other times the visitor whose estate was deemed to be suitably exalted was entertained to meals in the Great Chamber, while guests of slightly lower estate sat in the Hall, at the high table where the steward presided in lieu of his master. In a noble household the steward himself was a member of a gentry family, as were all the upper household officials who served a great lord in mediaeval times. In very large households an additional social gradation was made in the Great Chamber itself, where a second table was set up, called the 'knights' board', at which dined those guests too exalted to eat with the steward, yet not sufficiently so to join the lord himself and his guests of honour at the principal table. The social barrier between the Hall and the Great Chamber was significant and the appetite of the visitors who did not pass beyond the Hall may well have been affected by their chagrin as they looked about them and took in the fact that they were sitting alongside the steward, and not in the Chamber with his master. It is not surprising that protests were sometimes made, like the letter written by Mr. Marlivale of Chevington to his neighbour Sir Thomas Kytson (1485–1540) of Hengrave, complaining that when he visited Hengrave Hall he dined at the steward's table in the Hall, and not in the Great Chamber.[11]

Although they no longer ate under the eyes of their entire household, the lord and lady had little opportunity to relax informally over their meal in the Great Chamber. Even when no guests were with them, the sewer, the carver, the cupbearer and their attendant grooms all had to be present. A procession of these household officers carried the cooked dishes from the kitchen, first traversing the Hall where the lower orders rose respectfully to their feet, bared their heads, and stood in silence while the cortège with its burden of food passed through.[12] The dishes were then transported to the Chamber, reached from the dais end of the Hall and very often on a higher level, so the bearers had to climb a staircase before they could enter it; and finally the tepid food was served to the lord and lady and any guests who might be with them with virtually as much ritual as attended the service of large formal feasts in the Hall.

Precedence was as important as ever when it came to the seating and serving of the company in the Chamber. The person of highest estate, whether host or guest, sat in the grandest chair, often under a canopy (in the High Great Chamber at Hardwick Hall the original canopy survived *in situ* into the nineteenth century, when it was removed and replaced by a new one[13]). Much of the meal was passed in silence, partly because the rules of precedence strictly defined who might speak first to whom, thus inhibiting spontaneous conversation, and partly because the presence of the serving staff inhibited it still further.[14] The company could therefore concentrate upon looking about the room; and through its furnishings the host could demonstrate his wealth and his ability to live in the manner appropriate to his estate to guests whose own estate was not dissimilar to his.

The Great Chamber continued in use as an eating place for a surprisingly long time, in a few houses until as late as the second half of the seventeenth century. The furnishings of the mediaeval Chamber echoed those of the Hall on a feast day, with sumptuous tapestries, hangings and draped cloths as the most noticeable features. Furnishings began to change following the accession of Henry Tudor in 1485, when high-ranking

The Great Chamber of Tudor and Stuart times

families abandoned their custom of moving from castle to castle during the year. England was at last at peace, and they could settle down in one principal castle or manor house, and use the money which had formerly paid for personal armies and other expenses of war to improve and enrich their homes. Existing buildings were extended, and eventually many families built themselves grand new country houses; and they also improved and modernised their furnishings.

In the Great Chamber permanently fixed tapestries and wainscot panelling replaced temporary wall-hangings. The fireplace was given a magnificently carved chimneypiece. The bed remained in position in the Chamber until late in the sixteenth century, and even later in a few houses; but eventually it was moved to a separate bedchamber, often situated beyond the Great Chamber and its adjacent withdrawing room. Indeed, there was one type of entertainment for which the bed and the eating and drinking facilities of the Chamber could be brought into play together. When the lying-in of the lord's wife took place after the birth of a new baby, her female friends came visiting to bring her gifts and see the baby. She sat up in bed, with its rich canopy and hangings, while they seated themselves on stools or chairs around her, to chat and partake of the wine and sweet-meats which always had to be prepared well ahead when a lying-in was in prospect.

The table was no longer a board on trestles, but a framed table; and a popular version for the use of diners was the drawleaf table, first introduced from Holland soon after the middle of the sixteenth century: this could be extended by means of its extra leaves to accommodate a larger company when required. Additional small tables were placed within the Chamber, covered by the newly fashionable turkey carpet, or by a 'table-carpet' of velvet or heavy woollen cloth edged with fringing. The cupboard was still the place where silver vessels were displayed on

2.
Court cupboard, walnut, *c.* 1600. Originally this example was supported by four low feet beneath the bottom tier (R. Fastnedge, *English Furniture Styles*, p.39).

tiered shelves, and where wine and wine-cups were set in readiness. But its tiers no longer rose behind a flat board on trestles. The Tudor and Stuart 'court cupboard' was formed of three open tiers, with wine and wine-cups placed on the top tier, the largest pieces of silver displayed on the lowest tier, and the middle one either used for similar displays or else closed in with carved panels of woodwork and one or two doors, to provide storage space for valuable objects.

Chairs and stools were less heavy than in former times, and were often ornamentally carved. After the sawmill came into use, joiners responded by increasing their skills both in the construction of furniture and in decorative wood-carving. By the Elizabethan era, some chairs and stools were being given upholstered seats and backs,

3.
Joined stool, oak, late
sixteenth century, (R.
W. Symonds, 'The
"dyning parlor" and its
furniture', p.14).

though the art of upholstery was still in its infancy, and
the padding was not always arranged to the best
advantage for comfort. Those that lacked upholstery were
decorated with intricate carving or with inlaid wood if
they were intended for the Great Chamber; and some of
the cushions of rich materials listed in Tudor and Stuart
inventories must have helped to ease the hardness of the
wood. A few more chairs now made their appearance in
the Great Chamber, but they were still outnumbered by
the stools upon which all but the most distinguished
guests sat at table when meals were served there.

Just how magnificently a Great Chamber might be
furnished can be seen from the 1601 inventory of
Hardwick Hall. The house was built in the 1590s by the
Countess of Shrewsbury, the richest woman in England
after the Queen, and boasted two Great Chambers, one
on the second floor and one on the first. The contents of
the Low Great Chamber included:

Eight pieces of tapestry hangings of the story of
David eleven foot deep, a long table carved and
inlaid, two long turkey carpets for it, a square
table set with marble stones & inlaid with black
and white wood, another square table, a square
turkey carpet for it, a cupboard, two turkey carpets
for it, one of them with my lady's arms in it, a
chair of cloth of gold and silver with a fret
[interlaced work] of green velvet and with green
silk fringe, a chair of mulberry and yellow velvet
with gold and red silk fringe, a chair of yellow
satin ... two little chairs of crimson velvet with
gold fringe, a footstool of wood, a foot carpet of
turkey work, eight stools of black and white kersey
[coarse wool cloth] embroidered with needlework
flowers with red and black silk fringe, a low stool
of cloth of gold and silver with a fret of green
velvet and with a green silk fringe, a little inlaid
stool, two forms of cloth of gold with a border of
green velvet and gold fringe, a form of cloth of
silver with a border of green velvet and gold
fringe, a form of yellow damask with a border of
crimson velvet and gold fringe, one long cushion
of cloth of gold with a gold fringe and lined with
russet satin . . ..[15]

Six further cushions equally magnificent in their materials
and trimmings, green Penistone [heavy woollen fabric]
curtains for the windows, a number of paintings – all
portraits except for one of the Virgin Mary, a looking-glass
with 'his [the Earl of Shrewsbury's] and my ladies arms' set
in it, several additional tables, and fireplace furniture, are
all duly recorded in the rest of the entry.

Other very grand houses came near to matching this
rich array; and lesser ones would have had Great
Chambers furnished with several items similar to those
listed here, even if their upholstery was less dazzling and

their painted portraits were fewer. The Chamber in the house of any wealthy household was a showcase, described in a set of household regulations of the period as the place 'where the lord keepeth his presence, and the eyes of the best sort of strangers be there lookers on.'[16]

The reactions of the 'best sort of strangers' as they gazed around them were rather different from those of the earlier feasters in the mediaeval hall. The visitors eating in the Great Chamber of the Tudor and early Stuart era were looking about, judging, criticising, discovering what was new, with a view to acquiring furnishings as good or even better if they could afford them for their own Great Chambers. For the rules of precedence were breaking down. Great lords were now prepared to entertain in their Chambers men whose wealth, ability or influence compensated for their lowlier estate. New fashions spread quite quickly from the nobility to the gentry and to the families of successful merchants and farmers. William Harrison noted this phenomenon more than once, for instance in the case of Venetian glass from Murano which 'our gentilitie' had recently come to prefer to silver and silver-gilt for their drinking vessels: 'And as this is seen in the gentilitie, so in the wealthie communalitie the like desire of glass is not neglected'. And the fashion spread right down the social scale, reaching even the poorest who could not afford Venetian glass, so 'they content themselves with such as is made at home of fern and burnt stone'.[17]

Harrison made similar comments upon the 'abundance of Arras, rich hangings of tapestry, silver vessels and as much other plate as may furnish sundry cupboards' to the value of one or two thousand pounds in noblemen's houses; the 'tapestry, turkeywork, pewter, brass, fine linen, and thereto costly cupboards of plate worth five or six hundred pounds' in the houses of knights, gentlemen and merchants; and the way in which 'inferior artificers and many farmers' had in turn begun to 'garnish their cupboards with plate, their beds with tapestry and silk hangings and their tables with fine napery'.[18] Mediaeval homes at all levels had been sparsely furnished compared with the many new household objects now being acquired by everybody who could afford them.

The plate and tapestries decked the Great Chambers of the nobility and upper gentry. But not all gentry houses boasted a Great Chamber. Smaller manor houses of late mediaeval and Tudor times sometimes had just a 'privy parlour' behind the Hall which contained the owner's bed, as well as the table, chair, stools and cupboard which allowed it to be used as an eating room.

Documents of the sixteenth century refer occasionally to the 'dining parlour' or 'dining chamber'. This was the first time that a room had been specifically designated as an eating place, and it was often a new room added to an existing house, or included in the plan of a new house designed to contain also either a Great Chamber or a parlour.[19] In the greater houses it was the room used by the family when they wished to dine informally alone or with one or two close friends without the pomp which attended meals in both the Hall and the Great Chamber. The difference can be seen reflected in the relatively simple furnishings of the Little Dining Chamber at Hardwick Hall ('a long drawing [drawleaf] table, a turkey carpet for it, a chair of turkey-work, a stool of turkey-work, fourteen joined stools [separate wooden stools made by a joiner], a fire-shovel, a pair of tongs, wainscot round the same room) when compared with the magnificent furniture and decorations in the Low and High Great Chambers.[20] Where houses still had no named dining chamber, the lord and his wife sometimes dined informally in the withdrawing chamber off the Great Chamber.

During the seventeenth century substantial changes were made in the planning of the English country house,

The dining parlour and the dining-room

4.
Side table, mahogany,
c. 1730, in Lady Lever
Art Gallery, Port
Sunlight.

and towards the end of the century the dining-room was beginning to take its place as the principal eating room. In the newest houses, the hall was built on a smaller scale than formerly. Though still the large imposing entrance-room of the house, it was no longer the usual eating-place for the lower ranks of the household, nor were feasts held there in the mediaeval fashion.

The servants were relegated to a hall of their own for their meals, close to the kitchen and other food offices, and situated a storey below the entrance-hall. This segregation reflected a change in the status of the servants themselves. They were no longer members of noble and gentry families, only a little lower in their estate than the lords on whom they waited, but people of the middling sort – sons of clergymen, army officers and lawyers. Their place was soon taken by footmen (originally employed to run alongside the carriages of the gentry families, and to carry messages for them; then brought indoors to serve at the second table in the Great Chamber on days when the family were at home entertaining visitors; and finally transferred to dining-room duties when that room had become the place where the family and their guests usually ate their main meals).[21]

In the seventeenth-century house the lowest floor containing the kitchen and the servants' hall was still at garden level, with the rest of the house above. A grand

5.
Side table, urns, pedestals and wine cooler in mahogany made *c.* 1776 by Thomas Chippendale for Paxton House, Berwickshire.

flight of external steps was constructed to lead up from the garden to the doorway of the entrance-hall, while an internal staircase allowed the servants to reach the rooms off that hall. The saloon, often placed directly behind the entrance-hall, took the place of the Great Chamber as the most important reception room. The family dining parlour or little dining-room on the same floor began to increase in size and importance. In the smaller manor house, the three principal rooms on the entrance floor were hall, parlour and dining parlour.

Typical furnishings for a dining-room in the second half of the seventeenth century are listed by Randle Holme in *The Academy of Armoury* (published at Chester in 1688, though the draft manuscript version is dated 1649). The dining-room was to be:

> 'well wainscotted about ... The room hung with pictures of all sorts ... long table in the middle, either square to draw out in leaves, or long, or round, or oval with falling leaves. Side tables or court cupboards for cups and glasses to drink in, spoons, sugar box, phials and cruses for vinegar, oil and mustard pot. Cistern of brass, pewter or lead to set flagons of beer and bottles of wine in. A Turkey table cover or carpet of cloth or leather

printed. Chairs and stools of Turkey work, Russia or calves' leather, cloth or stuff or of needlework. Or else made all of joint work [i.e. wood] or cane chairs ... and a large seeing glass at the high end of the room.[22]

Gate-legged tables had become a popular alternative to draw-leaf tables, either in the form of a single large round or oval table, or as a group of two or three smaller straight-sided tables plus two rounded ones which could be opened up in such a way as to form a long table with curved ends to seat a large company. The various curved tables were especially suitable for the family dining parlour or dining-room where only a few close friends or relatives were present as visitors. Everyone was fully aware of the 'estate' of everyone else, and all were at ease with one another, so there was no need for the host or principal guests to be defined by the position or style of their seats at the table. People of both sexes were present, and wives often accompanied their husbands on visits. Moreoever, when people sat all around the table, conversation could be more informal, across the table as well as on either side of each diner.

Randle Holme mentioned chairs and stools uphol-stered in a variety of ways. The armless dining-chair of the seventeenth century was also known as a backstool (and in modern times as a 'farthingale chair' because in the parlour such chairs were often seats for women). It had a straight, not very high, back which might be decorated with carving, and its four legs were linked by stretchers near ground level, like those of the joined stool. Later in the century, backstools were often upholstered in cloth or leather to match the dining-chairs with arms and the stools in the dining parlour or dining-room. Six armchairs covered with crimson velvet and '12 backstools of the same' appear in the 1677 inventory of furnishings for the Great Dining Room (equivalent of the former Great

Chamber) at Ham House²³ In the same room, 8 cedar
tables were listed in the 1679 inventory (and 11 in 1683),
which may have been folding tables kept behind the
Indian screens also in the room, and set up together to
form bigger tables of various sizes when needed. Except at
mealtimes, the chairs and backstools would have stood
around the walls.

Holme had several types of upholstery for his chairs,
including two sorts of leather. Gilt leather was a
fashionable furnishing fabric in the later seventeenth
century, used for wall-hangings as well as chairs, as for
instance in the Marble Dining Room, which was part of a
new sequence of ground-floor rooms added to Ham
House in the 1670s.²⁴ People believed that leather was less
prone to pick up and hold food smells than tapestry
hangings and cloth upholstery; and it was grander than
simple wainscot.

Holme's list of furnishings also shows that the court
cupboard was about to be superseded by the side-table as
a place to hold drinking vessels. Side-tables carried
decoration of inlaid or carved wood just below their tops
on three sides only; the fourth, left plain, stood against a
wall. His dining-room is in fact very much a showcase
room, with its pictures and looking-glass and its
upholstered chairs and stools; and the new-fangled *cistern*
to keep bottles cool which was soon to be given the
special name of *cellaret*. In a smaller country house this
room would undoubtedly have been the one in which the
most important guests were entertained to dinner: the
informal, casual family eating would have taken place in
the parlour. The larger houses vacillated for a time
between the former Great Chamber, sometimes
rechristened the Great Dining Room (as at Ham House),
and a usually smaller and more recently built room for
family dining which might however contain newer, more
fashionable furniture than the large Chamber. In the
eighteenth century this dilemma was resolved by having a

single grand dining-room as one of a series of rooms grouped around the hall on the entrance level.

To meet the fashionable demand for carved furniture the cabinet-maker's art was making great advances at this period. This was due in part to the influence of a number of Dutch cabinet-makers who came to England in the reign of William and Mary.

The eighteenth-century country house dining-room Eighteenth-century dining-rooms are not unfamiliar to us today, as many country houses open to the public were either built or expanded and re-designed in that century. In most of them a suite of rooms arranged around three sides of the hall on the entrance floor included both a dining-room and a drawing-room. Both were large, important rooms, often set symmetrically opposite one another across the hall. This arrangement had the advantage of muffling the loud conversation of the men who sat long over their after-dinner port, so that it did not impinge too much upon the ladies chatting in the drawing-room.[25]

The typical eighteenth-century dining-table was large, and was made of mahogany, a wood which came into fashion due to the scarcity of French walnut in the 1720s.[26] Dinner-tables of the Georgian period were often constructed with a flap, either rectangular or curved. This single flap served to extend the table; and two medium-sized flap-tables could be put together to make one long one, or a rectangular centre unit with two extension flaps could be further extended by two semicircular ends which would stand against the wall as side-tables when not in use for dining. The dining-room was carpeted, and the table or tables did not remain *in situ* when the meal was over. They were moved aside, and sometimes stored outside the room altogether, in a corridor or nearby lobby.[27] The gleaming expanse of mahogany visible in the middle of the eighteenth-century dining-room in today's stately home does not give an authentic impression of how the room would have looked then. After the diners had left their seats, the chairs were also moved away from the centre, and were ranged around the sides of the room with their backs to the walls, so that people passing through or pausing to sit at the edge of the room to converse, could appreciate the appearance of the carpet as well as other aspects of the decor.

The cane dining-chairs mentioned by Randle Holme continued to be popular in the early Georgian period as did chairs of walnut or mahogany with upholstered seats and, often, backs of openwork wood with the central splat and the side-rails handsomely carved. As the century progressed, the cane chairs fell out of favour, while the carved-wood chairs were given lighter, more intricately designed backs; examples of some of the finest Chippendale, Hepplewhite and Sheraton chairs still exist. There was great variety in their appearance as Palladian, French, Gothick and Chinese design influenced both chair-makers and cabinet-makers.

Side-tables, which had replaced the earlier court cupboards, could be heavily decorated with swags of flowers and fruit; or with vines and heads of Bacchus to act as a reminder that wine was served from the table-top. Below, at floor level, stood the cellaret to contain the wine bottles. Later in the century a more austere classical revival influenced the decoration of the tables, but they were flanked by additions in the form of a pair of urns on pedestals designed to match them: this fashion may have originated with Robert Adam. Hepplewhite recommended that one pedestal be lined with tin and contain a stand for a heater and racks on which plates could be warmed. The other pedestal was to be a cupboard for pots; or it could be fitted with a drawer lined with lead to act as a sink where the butler rinsed the glasses. The urns were fitted with taps, one containing water for the rinsing operation, while the other might hold iced water for drinking. An alternative form of the side-table, pictured in

Hepplewhite's *The Cabinet-makers and Upholsterers Guide* (3rd edition, 1794) was a table with a curved or serpentine front and deep drawers at the side fitted to contain plates and cloths and a bottle-rack. One was lined with lead to hold the water for rinsing the glasses and cutlery, as in the eighteenth century it was customary for both to be washed in the dining-room.[28]

A different type of side-table, found in drawing-rooms and salons as well as in dining-rooms, was the pier-table, set beneath the pier-glass. Pier-glasses were very much an indicator of the well-furnished country house in the eighteenth century; they were often arranged in pairs, with the window-casement between them.

Wall decorations of gilt leather set into wooden panelling began to go out of fashion about 1710. Wallpapers, which initially imitated fabrics, were first made in London about 1700. Wooden wainscot, wallpaper or, later, smooth plaster or stucco covered the walls. Robert Adam wrote in 1773 of dining-rooms: 'Instead of being hung with damask, tapestry &c., they are always finished with stucco and adorned with statues and paintings, that they may not retain the smell of the victuals.'[29]

The guest who ate in the dining-room and gazed about the room, admiring the chairs, the side-tables and the pierglasses, the elaborate plasterwork of the ceiling, hardly needed to make enquiries about their origin. Architects and cabinet-makers were producing their own catalogues from at least the 1740s, so new design ideas circulated quite quickly in the world of country-house owners, who could buy or borrow copies of these books; and could then ask their own joiners to reproduce pieces of furniture they particularly liked. And many new furniture designs were created in the eighteenth century, to meet the needs of country-house life.

Conversation flowed easily at the dining-table, and was limited only by the presence of the footman-waiters.

About 1740 an English invention, the *dumb waiter*, was added to dining-room furniture. In its most usual form it comprised a set of three circular trays which revolved about a central stem on tripod-legs. A set of dumb waiters placed near the corners of the dining-table to hold the dessert meant that once the second-course dishes had been served out, the live waiters could be banished, and 'conversation was not under any restraint by the servants being in the room'.[30]

Other new furniture for the convenience of eaters and drinkers was not necessarily destined for the dining-room. When fireplaces became smaller towards the end of the century a semicircular or horseshoe-shaped wine-table was created, large enough to allow a group of drinkers to sit around the fire.[31] The most sophisticated models had a metal track, also semicircular, set around the shorter inner curve, along which the wine-bottle could travel, and also a short curtain hanging above the inner edge to keep the fire off the drinker's faces while they toasted their toes.

The breakfast parlour or breakfast-room emerged during the eighteenth century as a morning room where ladies could carry on various activities and the gentlemen could join them if the weather was bad enough to keep them from shooting or other outdoor occupations. For the use of those who ate there, a special breakfast-table was invented. It had a shelf below the top, often enclosed by a fretwork of wood; and when the meal was finished, the crockery and any other remains could be transferred to the shelf, thus freeing the table-top for other uses.[32]

The appetite, the eye and a new drink

Perhaps the most striking example of new equipment and furniture was that which accompanied the advent of a new drink: tea. The ceremony of tea-drinking was first popularised at the English court by Catherine of Braganza, wife of King Charles II. The custom had taken root earlier in Portugal, where tea had been arriving in small quantities from China since the middle of the sixteenth century.[33] The serving of tea was carried out by the hostess herself: she prepared the new drink by boiling water on a special small heater fuelled by spirits of wine, brewing it in a teapot, and pouring it into elegant little handleless cups of Chinese porcelain. The equipment was imported from the Far East; and rectangular Chinese or Javanese tea-tables with fretwork edgings were also introduced into some houses (the one at Ham House had its short legs lengthened with additional lower legs of barley-sugar-twisted wood by a joiner in England about 1680, to bring it to a height suitable for ladies seated on the average seventeenth-century backstool or armchair).[34] Soon after 1700 small round-topped tea-tables with a central column supported on tripod legs began to come into fashion.

Tea was served after dinner and after supper. As the hour for dinner moved gradually forward from 2 p.m. or 3 p.m. to 4 p.m. or 5 p.m. and eventually into the evening, ladies sometimes took tea and sweetmeats in the afternoon to help fill the gap before dinner. After-dinner tea was never prepared in the dining-room, but in some other part of the house – initially at one end of the Long Gallery; then, in some houses, in a small room equipped as a Tea Room and furnished with a spirit-heater, tea-table and often with other pieces of lacquer furniture. But in due course the drawing-room became the most usual venue for after-dinner tea-drinking, and the hostess brewed and served the drink only when the men finally 'joined the ladies' after their prolonged bout of port-drinking in the dining-room.[35]

The demand for tea, when it first became a fashionable drink, was fed very much by what the eye beheld in terms of its surroundings and the opportunity it gave for acquiring and using elegant new artefacts. The desire to emulate the hostess who offered tea to her guests made a strong impact on the ladies who partook of her hospitality and, as the price of leaf tea fell, the custom spread rapidly

6.
A family taking tea.
From a painting by R.
Colius, 1732, in the
Victoria & Albert
Museum, London.

through the ranks of society. The coffee-house, where
another very new drink was consumed, was the province
of the men; but coffee-drinking did not spread through
the nation, or make an impact within its lower ranks, on
the same scale as tea.[36]

In the mediaeval Hall the members of a male, still
partly warrior society beheld the food and its
surroundings, and their appetites were stimulated
through messages conveyed by all the splendour and
colour that they saw. In the seventeenth- and eighteenth-
century English country house, women shared the meals
and the mealtime conversations of their menfolk, and ate
with them in dining-rooms which had already developed
into recognisable forerunners of our dining-rooms today.
And in the new ritual of tea-drinking, it was the appetite
and eye of women which ensured the rapid progress of a
novel food custom through society.

Bibliography

P. Eames, *Furniture in England, France and the Netherlands from the Twelfth
to the Fifteenth Century* (London, 1977).
R. Fastnedge, *English Furniture Styles from 1500 to 1830* (London, 1962).
M. Girouard, *Life in the English Country House: a Social and Architectural
History* (New Haven and London, 1978).

E. Mercer, *Furniture 700–1700* (London, 1969).

P. Thornton, *Seventeenth-century Interior Decoration in England, France and Holland* (New Haven and London, 1978).

Notes and References

1. C. B. Hieatt & S. Butler, eds, *Curye on Inglysch* (Early English Text Society, SS 8, 1985) p.20.
2. R. W. Chambers, ed., *A Generall Rule to Teche Every Man ... to Serve a Lord or Mayster (British Library MS Add. 37969)* (Early English Text Society, OS 148, 1914) p.11.
3. Ibid., p.13.
4. Eames (1977) p.190.
5. Mercer (1969) pp.82–3.
6. Eames (1977) pp.56–7 and 256f (Appendix 8: Alienor de Poitiers, text). The cup-board became ever more impressive as the Middle Ages drew to a close, culminating in such ostentatious spectacles as that put on by Henry VIII when he gave a great feast for the French ambassadors in 1519: 'the cup-board in the Hall was of twelve stages, all of plate of gold and no gilt plate'. R. Holinshed, *Chronicle*, 894.a.40, quoted by R. Warner, *Antiquitates Culinariae* (London, 1791) p.xli.
7. See p.18.
8. B. A. Henisch, *Fast and Feast: Food in Mediaeval Society* (University Park, Pa., 1976) pp.56–7.
9. Girouard (1978) p.46.
10. W. Langland, *Piers Plowman*, B version, ed. G. Kane & E. T. Donaldson (London, 1975) Passus 10, lines 97–103.
11. R. W. Symonds, 'The "dyning parlor" and its furniture', *Connoisseur* 113 (1944), p.12.
12. Girouard (1978), p.47, based on British Library MS Harleian 6815.
13. J. Cornforth, *English Interiors 1790–1848* (London, 1978), p.24.
14. Girouard (1978), p.51.
15. 'The Hardwick Hall inventory of 1601 (text)', *Furniture History* 7 (1971), pp.30–1.
16. Girouard (1978), p.88; 'A Breviate touching the order and government of a nobleman's house, 1605', communicated by Sir J. Banks, *Archaeologia* 13 (1800), p.322.
17. W. Harrison, *Description of England*, ed. from Holinshed's *Chronicle* 1577 and 1587 by F. J. Furnivall (London, 1877), p.147.
18. Ibid. pp.238–9.
19. Symonds (1944), pp.12–13.
20. 'Hardwick Hall inventory, 1601', p.30.
21. Girouard (1978), pp.136–43.
22. R. Holme, *The Academy of Armoury 1688*, Bk. 3, ch. 16 = Roxburghe Club ed., 1905, vol. 2, pp.15–16; R. Edwards & L. G. G. Ramsay, eds., *The Connoisseur Complete Period Guides* (London, 1968), p.322, note.
23. P. Thornton & M. Tomlin, 'The furnishing and decoration of Ham House', *Furniture History* 16 (1980), pp.118–9. For further details of backstools, see Thornton (1978), pp.185–92.

24. Thornton & Tomlin (1980), pp.43–4.

25. Girouard (1978), pp.204–5.

26. Fastnedge (1962), p.113f.

27. Ibid., p.174; M. Tomlin, 'The 1782 inventory of Osterley Park', *Furniture History* 22 (1986), pp.120; 122 for dining table absent from dining-room and stored in lobby; J. Low, 'Newby Hall: two late eighteenth-century inventories', *Furniture History* 22 (1986), p.154 for dining tables stored under 'Great Stair Case'.

28. Fastnedge (1962), pp.207–8.

29. R. & J. Adam, *The Works in Architecture*, ed. R. Oresko (London, 1975), p.48, preface to Vol. I, i, plate 5.

30. Mary Hamilton, *Diary 1784*, in Fastnedge (1962), p.149.

31. *The Cabinet-Makers' London Book of Prices*, 2nd ed. (London, 1793) reprinted in *Furniture History* 18 (1986), p.102, describes with illustration 'A Gentleman's Social Table', an early version of this type of wine-table.

32. T. Chippendale, *The Gentleman and Cabinet-Maker's Director 1754*, new ed. (London, 1957) plate 53.

33. Initially through Portugal's trading-station at Macao. Tea began to reach England much later via the East Indies and Holland. Only in 1664 did the East India Company begin a small trade in leaf-tea direct with England.

34. Illustrated in Thornton (1978) p.229. It is possibly the 'tee table carved and guilt' in the Duchess of Lauderdale's private closet in the Ham House inventory of 1683. In the same room was 'One Japan [lacquered] box for sweetmeats & tee'. Thornton & Tomlin (1980) p.84. An early record of a heater is the entry added to the inventory of 1679 for 'One Indian furnace for tee garnish't wt silver' ['Indian' was the seventeenth-century term for 'oriental'] in the White Closet, next door to her private closet, where the Duchess presumably entertained her friends to afternoon tea. Here there were also 4 (later 6) armchairs of 'japan red'. Thornton & Tomlin (1980) p.79.

35. Girouard (1978) pp.204–5 plausibly connected the advent of tea-drinking with the development of the men's lengthy port-drinking sessions after the ladies left the dining-room. He thought this custom, unique to Britain, originated as 'a short practical interval in which the ladies retired to brew tea or coffee, after which the gentlemen joined them to drink it'.

36. In the second half of the eighteenth century tea became much cheaper, and it was then drunk even by labourers' families in the South of England, though they could still only afford teas of poor quality, often adulterated with leaves of local trees and by other means. They did not take to cheap adulterations of coffee (made from burnt crusts, dandelion roots, etc.). For them tea had an additional appeal as a hot drink to replace their former cold, small beer. The warmth of tea was a less important feature for the well-to-do, who had access to warm caudles, hot spiced ales etc.

4.

Decoration of the Tudor and Stuart Table

PETER BREARS

The sixteenth and seventeenth centuries encompass one of the most interesting phases of English culinary history, one which saw the transformation of the long-established mediaeval tradition into a recognisably modern form. This was particularly the case with regard to ceremonial, the methods of service, the dressing and presentation of the food, and the use of a whole range of new dining utensils.

Up to this period, the leading members of society all maintained large households, each peer having scores of retainers led by a series of household officers whose number, title and duties were exactly defined according to their master's rank. Even quite ordinary knights such as Sir Hugh Cholmley of Whitby had:

> between thirty and forty in my ordinary family, a
> chaplain who said prayers every morning at six
> and again before dinner and supper, a porter who
> merely attended the gates, which were ever shut
> up before dinner when the bell rang for prayers,
> and not opened till one o'clock, except for
> strangers who came to dinner, which was ever fit
> to receive three or four besides my family,
> without any trouble; whatever their fare was, they
> were sure of a hearty welcome. Twice a week, a

certain number of old people, widows and
indigent persons, were served at my gates with
bread and good pottage made of beef, which I
mention that those who succeed may follow the
example'.[1]

In general, the mediaeval practice was for great houses
to demonstrate their power and wealth by providing
plentiful, but plain, hospitality, based on substantial
pottages and good roasts.

In the mid-sixteenth century a number of great social
changes, especially the Dissolution of the Monas-
teries and the break with the Church of Rome, began
an exciting evolutionary period in England. The nobility and gentry, especially the Protestant élite
moving in court circles, were now demanding new
standards of splendour and comfort. Many members
of this group were self-made, their new fortunes being
drawn from redistributed monastic lands, from early
industrial activities, from commerce or from practising
the law. Like *nouveaux riches* the world over, they
felt the need to demonstrate their arrival on the social
scene with the most potent displays of wealth and power,
expressed in the form of vast, soaring houses, magnificent dress, and lavish entertainment. Their achievements were not celebrated in the chaste, muted
atmosphere of the classical tradition, but in a glorious
riot of colour, brightness, and complex linear pattern.
Symmetry and geometrical ingenuity characterise the
design of their great architectural façades, of their
gardens, and of their table-settings, these arrangements then being appropriately enriched. Masonry
received its flat, entwined strapwork and details
copied from continental pattern-books, box hedges
were planted and trimmed in complex geometric
knot-patterns, their interstices being filled with
colourful bedding plants to give a brilliant jewel-

like effect. Similar devices in pastry and fruit preserves soon appeared on the table in the form of pies, tarts and salads.

The relatively plain but very plentiful and open-handed hospitality of the mediaeval households contrasted greatly with the very rich and showy but relatively restricted fare of late Tudor and Stuart times. As Sir Henry Slingsby of Scriven commented:

> In former times the fashions were to keep great houses not affecting curiosity as plenty, [but now] they turn the honour of housekeeping into some one single entertainment for which our own marketts are too mean to afford them that which their curious appetites would have; but they must send beyond the sea to make trade of Merchants, only intend'd for public commodity, now at last serve their private ends of vain glory ... this abuse is not receiv'd by great personages of the nobility only, but even others, honoris gratia, must imitate even beyond their abilities will afford.[2]

The expense of the new life-style meant that the extended households who had dined in the hall with their lord were now dispersed, especially when the lord and his family now spent an ever-increasing period of the year in fashionable London. In addition, the practice of the lord and his family dining in their separate chamber or dining parlour, rather than in the hall, passed rapidly down the social scale to reach even the meanest gentry by the mid to late seventeenth century; and this change did away with all the mediaeval dining ceremonials, except in the greatest households in the land.

These developments altered every aspect of dining and so, in order to study each element in detail, we shall follow the progress of the meal from start to finish, noting en route the ceremonies, utensils and foods which created the rich visual effects so important in contemporary social life.

The first stage in preparing the table was to lay the tablecloth, this being either of damask, diaper, or hollands. In the first, the fine bleached white linen yarn was woven in elaborate twill designs which were revealed by the reflection of light. The Victoria and Albert Museum holds Elizabethan examples in which the Virgin Queen's portrait appears within an arched arcade, as well as those of the late seventeenth century, on which the Royal arms of William and Mary provide a beautiful all-over repeat pattern. The diaper cloths were similarly woven, but with a small, regular diamond pattern, while hollands were plain woven, also being used for shirts, coifs, towels or sheets. **The tablecloth**

In the early sixteenth century, the full mediaeval ceremonial approach to laying the cloth was still being maintained in the larger households, the following instructions to the butler being given in Wynkyn de Worde's *Book of Kervynge* of 1508:

> loke your table clothes, towelles and napkyns be
> fayre folden in a cheste or hanged upon a perche
> ... [then] when ye laye the clothe wype the
> borde cleane with a cloute, than laye a cloth [a
> couche it is called] take your felowe that one
> ende & holde you that other ende, than drawe
> the cloth strayght, the bought [i.e. fold or crease]
> on the utter edge, take the utter parte & hange it
> even, than take the thyrde cloth and laye the
> bought on the inner edge, and laye estat withall,
> the upper parte half a foot brode. Than cover thy
> cupborde and thyne ewery with the towell of
> dyapper ...

By these means, the table was covered with three cloths, each perhaps four to six yards in length.

Where the master of the household dined in his great chamber or dining chamber, an increasingly widespread practice throughout the sixteenth century, only a single cloth appears to have been laid, but the degree of ceremony was certainly maintained. In the house of a viscount, for example, the Gentleman Usher of the Great Chamber assembled the yeomen of the ewery, the pantry, the buttery and the cellar at the great chamber at 10 am, in order to prepare the table for dinner. After the Yeoman of the Ewery had prepared the ewery board, the Gentleman Usher then conducted him with due reverence:

> that is with two curtesies, one at the middest of
> the chamber, and an other att the table of my
> dyett: and that then kissing his hande he laye ytt
> on the middest of the table in the same place
> where the yeoman of the ewrye is to laye his
> cloth, the which he shall helpe to spreade. This
> service ended, and due curtesie doune, he shall
> return with him to the ewerye boorde.[3]

For the sovereign, however, the ceremonial reached its most extreme form in the reign of Queen Elizabeth, even though she was never present when it was performed. First two gentlemen entered the room, one bearing a rod, and the other a tablecloth, which, after they had both kneeled three times, with the utmost veneration, was then spread upon the table. After kneeling once more, they retired, to be succeeded by further gentlemen and ladies each bearing appropriate table furnishings and food.[4] By the time of William and Mary, this process started at 10 a.m. and 5 p.m. with the Gentleman Usher supervising the hand-washing of the cup-bearer, the carver and the sewer, then calling for a bowl of sack (a Spanish wine) to drink with one of these gentlemen before entering the Presence Chamber. Here they made their three 'congees' or bows at different parts of the chamber, and to the royal table, after which the carver directed the Yeoman of the Mouth in preparing the table for the forthcoming meal.[5]

After the cloth had been laid, it was set with all the necessary condiments, napkins and cutlery. Wynkyn de Worde instructed the butler:

> take thy towell aboute thy necke and laye that
> one syde of the towell upon thy lefte arme and
> there on lay your soveraynes napkyn and laye on
> thyne arme seven loves of brede with thre or
> foure trenchour loves with the ende of the towell
> in the lefte hande as in the maner is, than take
> thy salte seller in thy lefte hande and take the
> ende of the towell in your right hande to bere in
> spones and knyves.

Of these articles, the most important by far was the salt. **The salt**

> Thenne here-uppon the boteler or panter shall
> bring forthe his pryncipall salte ... he shall sette
> the saler in the myddys of the tabull accordyng
> to the place where the principall soverain shall
> sette ... thenne the seconde salte att the lower
> ende ... then salte selers shall be sette uppon the
> syde-tablys.

The principal salt described here in *Ffor to Serve a Lord* of 1500, was the most important piece of gold plate in the household, lavish in its materials, scale and quality of enrichment. In the late mediaeval period, it could take the form of dogs, elephants, lions or dragons, garnished with pearls, precious stones or enamels. Later it adopted an 'hour-glass' profile (*c.* 1480–1525), a cylindrical shape (*c.* 1550–1600), and a bell shape (*c.* 1580–1620), the latter developing into the spool-shaped pulley salt from *c.* 1625, which had three short scrolls rising above it to hold a plate in lieu of a cover. These salts were chiefly of ceremonial rather than practical use, for their place on the table effectively separated the lord and his chief guests from the

7.
Pottery Salts.
Salts made of lead-glazed earthenware were used in households where those of precious metals were far too expensive. The salts seen here were made in (A) 'Cistercian' ware in Yorkshire in the mid sixteenth century; (B) in 'Tudor Green' ware in Surrey in the late sixteenth or early seventeenth century; and (C) in mid-sixteenth century yellow-glazed 'Reversed Cistercian' ware: this one was excavated from Sandal Castle near Wakefield.

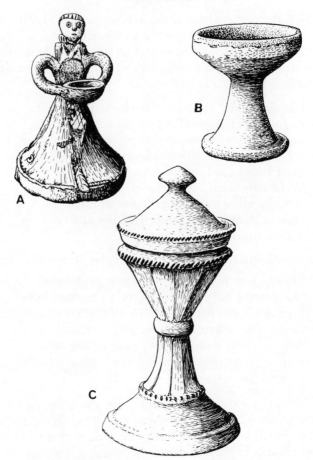

remainder of the diners. As late as the mid-seventeenth century, for example, Lord Fairfax was instructing his servants to 'let the best fashioned and apparelled servants attend above the salte, the rest belowe'.[6] From this time, however, the great salt slowly passed out of use as this manner of communal dining came to an end.

Smaller salts for individual use continued to be made throughout the seventeenth century and beyond,

8.

Silver Salts
The salt was the most significant piece of plate on the table, where it divided the most important diners from those 'below the salt'. These examples illustrate (A) an 'hourglass' salt at New College, Oxford, of 1493; (B) a 'bell' salt from Christ's Hospital, London, of 1607; (C) the cylindrical salt of the London Clothworkers Company of 1661; and (D) a 'pulley' salt at Mercers' Hall, London of 1685.

triangular forms with a central circular depression for the salt being popular from the 1620s. Circular or polygonal varieties were also made from the 1630s. It was probably a salt of this type which Samuel Pepys noted in his diary for October 29th, 1663, when he found that 'Under every salt there was a bill of fare'.

9.

A Perfect School for Officers of the Mouth of 1682 gives detailed instructions for folding napkins. To form a Cockleshell Double (top), take the open napkin (A) and fold 'in bands' as seen in (B). Tightly pleat the napkin at right-angles to the bands (C), then use a blunt point to lift up each folding edge of the bands (D) nipping them firmly into place. Finally turn the napkin upside down, squeeze up the central pleats and place a dinner bun on them before raising up the fan-like shells at back and front (E). To make a Cross (below), take the flat napkin (A) and fold the corners to the centre before turning over (B) and folding the points to the centre once more. Turn the napkin over then fold up each corner (C) to produce a Cross (D). To make a Cross of Lorraine, turn the napkin over (E) and pull up the corners before inserting the dinner bun (F).

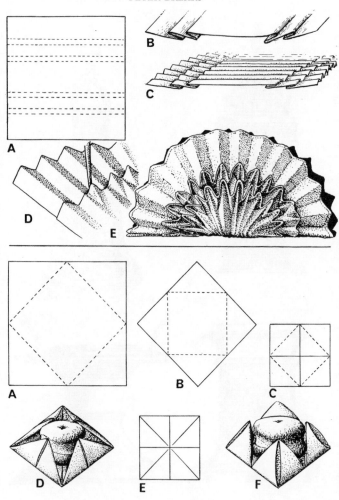

Where expensive silver salts were beyond the means of the household, their place was taken by examples made either in pewter or in glazed pottery. As early as the late fifteenth century, potters in Yorkshire were making cup-salts in yellow lead-glazed earthenware, their pedestals

64

being given knife-cut facets in imitation of silverware. (I excavated one of these from the floor of the great hall at Haselden Hall in Wakefield in 1967). Further examples were made in the Coventry area, as well as in the potteries of the Hampshire-Surrey border, the latter being supplied to the Inns of Court and Basing House near Basingstoke. From the early mid-seventeenth century the London delftware potters also made salts, some of which copied the pulley shape of contemporary silverware, while others had hemispherical cups mounted on broad conical bases.[7]

Napkins of linen cloth, either plain or diaper, or damask, **Napkins** were usually about a yard square. They were laid, according to *The Book of Kervynge* of 1508, 'fayre folden besyde your brede'.

The same source describes the methods to be used:

> yf ye wyll wrappe youre soveraynes brede stately
> ye muste square and proporcyon youre brede and
> se that no lofe be more than an other, and than
> shall ye make your wrapper manly, than take a
> towel of reynes of two yerdes and a halfe and
> take the towell by the endes double and laye it
> on the table, than take the ende of the bought
> [fold] a handfull in your hande and wrappe it
> harde and laye the ende soo wrapped betwene
> two towelles upon that ende so wrapped laye
> your brede botom to botom syxe or seven loves,
> than set youre brede manerly in fourme.

Detailed descriptions regarding the folding of the napkin do not appear to have been printed in this country until 1682, when *A Perfect School of Instructions for the Officers of the Mouth* was issued.[8] Here most of the imaginative designs, ranging from napkins in the form of a Hen and Chickens to those "in the form of two Capons in a Pye" were also intended to enclose a round bread roll, although

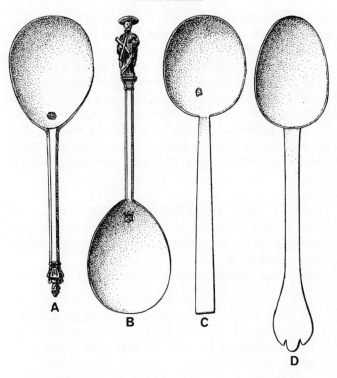

Spoons others, such as "An excellent Heart" were purely decorative.

Spoons were used to eat all the liquid and semi-liquid foods which appeared on the mediaeval and post-mediaeval table, especially the pottages and dishes served on moist sops of bread so popular before the introduction of dining forks;[9]

An whenne your potage yow shall be brouhte,
Take yow sponys and soupe by no way,
And in youre dysshe leve nat your spone, I pray.

In all fashionable households, the spoons were made of silver or silver-gilt, their shallow fig-shaped bowls usually having fine rectangular- or hexagonal-sectioned stems terminating in knobs formed as an acorn (*c.* 1300–1550), wrythen, or spirally fluted (*c.* 1350–1559), a baluster (*c.* 1350–1625), a maidenhead (15th century–*c.* 1625), a lion (15th–early 17th century), a Moor's head (to 16th century), or a seal-top (late 16th–mid-17th century). Further spoons had their finials cast as apostles (*c.* 1450–1650) or worthies (16th–17th centuries), the latter depicting biblical, classical, historical, or romantic heroes. Unique designs were also made with their finials showing devices taken from their owners' heraldic achievements, Thomas Lord Wharton of Healaugh having 'towe gilte spones with the bulls head on the endes, tow white spones with a mawnske on the endes [and] one Dosane white spones with helmettes on the ende'.[10] In contrast, the slip-topped spoons made *c.* 1500–1650 had no finials, the tops of their stems being neatly cut off at a slight angle.

From around *c.* 1660 spoons began to be made with oval bowls strengthened by a single rib running down the back. Their handles were broad and flat, especially at the end, which was formed into the three lobes and earned them the title of 'trifid' spoons. This area provided an ideal space for the ornate stamped or exquisite engraved decoration which is found on all the finest examples.

Knives

When dining on the joints of roasted and boiled meats which formed such a substantial part of the mediaeval and early post-mediaeval meal, each person used their long, sharp-pointed knife to cut off the pieces they required, manners dictating that they held the joint with no more than two fingers and a thumb while this was being done. The knife point was then used to transfer the meat onto the trencher, where it was sliced, as well as to take salt from the cellar as required.

The ordinary man carried his knife in a sheath attached

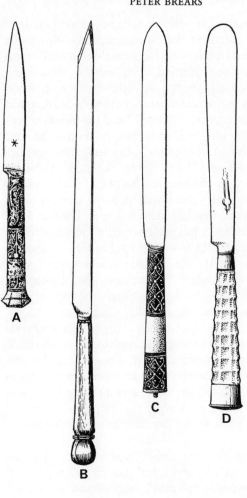

11.
Knives
As forks came into use, the knives dispensed with their sharp points which had formerly been necessary for spearing food from the chargers. This is shown in these examples of *c.* 1530 (A); *c.* 1580 (B); *c.* 1630 (C); *c.* 1670, by Thomas Eliott of London (D), and *c.* 1710 (E).

A

B

C

D

E

68

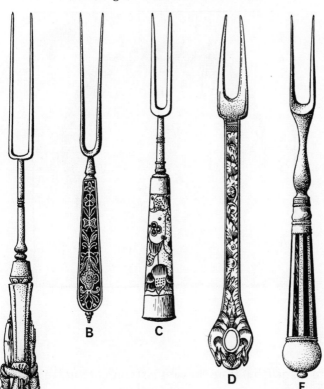

12.
Forks
Although some dining forks were used in England from the early seventeenth century, their real popularity commenced in the 1660s. These forks show carved ivory handles, *c.* 1670 (A); enamelled handles *c.* 1670 (B); ivory handles with inlaid silver and red and green stained decoration, *c.* 1670 (C); flat trifid handles with engraved decoration made by Thomas Mangy of York, *c.* 1680 (D), and ivory handles inlaid with tortoiseshell panels, *c.* 1710 (E).

A   B   C   D   E

13.
Trenchers
The example on the left, made of wood, has a broad, shallow central hollow for the meat etc., with a small hollow in one corner to hold the salt. It dates from the late sixteenth or early seventeenth century. The example on the right is of pewter with a wriggle-work portrait of William III, *c.* 1690s.

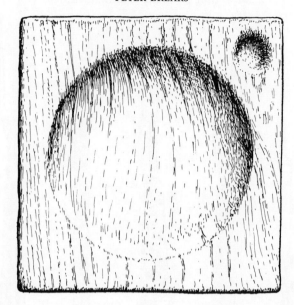

to his belt, but from the early sixteenth century the major households were providing cased sets of matching knives for the use of their guests. Perhaps the most magnificent of these was that owned by Henry VIII which was described in his inventory as:

> One woman of silver and gilt being a case of knives garnished with sundry emeralds and pearls and rubies about the neck and divers amethysts, jacynths and balases upon the foot thereof furnished with knives having diamonds at the ends of them.[11]

Other sets of his knives were accompanied by a single matching fork. This was not intended for eating, however, but was provided as a means of serving the meat.

The knives of the fifteenth and early sixteenth centuries measured some 6 to 7½ inches in length, both the cutting and the back edges usually having a gentle convex curve, while the handle was built up from two simple scales of wood, brass, bone or horn fixed to the tang with brass rivets. During the latter half of the sixteenth century the overall length of the knives extended up to 9½ inches, their blades being narrow, straight-backed, with a parallel cutting edge, and sharp point. Over the next fifty years they shrank again to around 7 or 8 inches, with parallel-sided triangular-tipped blades. The handles of these knives usually had a slightly tapering hexagonal or octagonal section, elegantly constructed with small panels or fillets of amber, ivory, agate or bone, perhaps enriched with silver filigree on the finer examples. In the latter half of the seventeenth century knives lost their sharp points, since forks had now taken over their role of spearing meat and transferring it to the mouth. Now the blades developed a bold convex curvature, their tips at first having either a rounded or almost square profile, then progressing to a full, round, almost scroll-like shape. The shorter and stouter handles, meanwhile, continued to be made in exotic materials such as agate, crystal, jet, enamel, or amber, with ivory examples decorated with red and green staining and inlaid silver wire becoming popular towards the end of the period.

Forks The fork, which we now take for granted as an essential utensil when dining, was only used by the greatest in the land during the mediaeval period, and then only for eating sticky suckets or sweetmeats. The references in *Bury Wills* to 'my silver forke for grene gyngour' of 1463 or 'my spoon with a forke in the end' of 1554, are to sucket forks of this type.[12] By the early sixteenth century the use of forks was beginning to spread into the main courses of dinner and supper, Ben Jonson noting in 1607 'Then must you learn the use And handling your silver fork at meals'.[13] The man usually credited with the introduction of the fork into English society was Tom Coryat, describing this continental fashion in his *Crudities* of 1611:

> The Italian and also most strangers that are commorant in Italy, doe alwaies at their meales use a little forke, when they cut their meate. For while with their knife which they hold in one hand they cut the meat out of the dish, they fasten their forke, which they hold in their other hand upon the same dish . . . their forkes being for the most part made of yron or steele and some of silver. The reason of this their curiosity

is, because the Italian cannot by any means
indure to have his dish touched with fingers,
seeing all men's fingers are not alike clean.
Hereupon I myself thought good to imitate the
Italian fashion by this forked cutting of meate,
not only while I was in Italy, but also . . . in
England since I came home.[14]

His optimism was not shared by others, Fynes Moryson
advising the travelled Englishman to 'lay aside the spoone
and forke of Italy, the affected gestures of France',[15] but
common sense and practicality prevailed, especially when
it was realised that if the diner's hands remained free from
meat juices, fish oils, sauces and similar messy and
odoriferous substances, the fine diaper napkins remained
relatively clean and unsoiled. By 1616 Jonson was asking:

Forks! what be they?
The laudable use of forks,
Brought into custom here, as they are in Italy,
To the sparing of napkins.

Even so, half a century was to pass before they were
generally accepted by the gentry, while almost three
centuries later they were only just being adopted by naval
ratings, farm servants and other sections of the working
classes.

Most of the forks made in the latter half of the
seventeenth century were made with long, two-pronged
hafts fitted with elongated conical handles bearing
identical decoration to that of their matching knives.
Silver provided a popular material for the handles,
whether it was left plain, or decorated with brightly
coloured enamels. Ivory gave even greater scope for
ornamentation, being intricately carved into the form of
human figures, or geometrically faceted, while in its
simplest shape its smooth surface could be inlaid with
silver wire, and brightly stained in floral patterns in red

and green. From around 1680, one-piece silver forks were made in which the handles resembled those of contemporary spoons, their hafts being hammered to a flat, rectangular section, swelling to a wide, three-lobed 'trifid' terminal. Soon their two prongs were being replaced by three-pronged versions, these being the direct ancestors of the forks in everyday use today.

Trenchers 'They sette hemselfe atte dyner, & made trenchers of brede for to putte theyr mete upon'. In these words, Caxton describes the usual mediaeval practice of placing thick slices of four-day-old wholemeal bread before each guest to act as a plate, protecting the tablecloth from knife-cuts and the juices which ran from the food.[16] A detailed account of their preparation and serving is given in *The Book of Kervinge:*

> The kerver muste knowe the kervinge and the
> fayre handlynge of a knyfe ... your knyfe must
> be fayre and your handes muste be clene ... In
> the myddes of your honde set the hafte ... with
> two fyngers & a thombe kervynge of brede,
> layenge & voydynge of crommes with two fyngers
> and a thombe, than take your lofe in your lefte
> honde & holde your knyfe surely, embrewe not
> the table cloth, but wype upon youre napkyn,
> than take the trenchoure lofe in youre lefte
> honde and with the edge of your table knyfe take
> up your trenchours as nye the poynt as ye may,
> than laye foure trenchoures to your soverayne
> one by an other, and laye theron other foure
> trenchoures or elles twayne ...

Trenchers of this kind can be seen before the diners in the 1596 painting of *The Life and Death of Sir Henry Unton*.
During the sixteenth century the bread trencher disappeared, its place being taken by trenchers of wood or

metal. Wooden trenchers were already in use on the Earl of Northumberland's table in 1512, while Sir William Petre purchased three dozen for eighteen pence for Ingatestone Hall in Essex in 1561.[17] In shape, they were either square, like the bread trencher, or round, Baret describing 'A Trencher to eate meate on' as being 'a broad trencher [or] a Round trencher' in the late 1570s, while in 1624 Captain John Smith reported that the inhabitants of Virginia 'imagined the world to be flat and round, like a trencher'.[18] In the better-quality houses, these wooden trenchers were soon replaced by pewter, Hollingshead recording how 'For household furniture, in our days, old men may remember great improvements, as the exchange of treene (i.e. wooden) platters for pewter, and wooden spoones for silver or tin'.[19] In many of the servants' halls, the farmhouses and cottages of England, however, the wooden trencher continued in use through to the opening years of the present century.

Pewter made of tin alloyed with copper had been used in England during the mediaeval period, the ordinances of the Pewterers' Company of London of 1348 mentioning chargers, saucers and salt-cellars. A table of weights of pewterware prepared in 1438 suggests that by this time chargers were being made over thirteen inches in diameter, platters from eight to thirteen inches, and dishes and saucers down to four inches. Although most of these articles were used for serving the food, the platters could also have been used for dining. Even so, the first documentary evidence of that practice appears to be an entry in the Pewterers' Company accounts for 1533–4, when, 'ii doss Trenchers ... waying xviii lbs at vi d. per lb' cost nine shillings, these details suggesting a diameter of some seven or eight inches.[20] Their plain rims were probably slightly hollow or cupped, with similar proportions to those of a modern dinner plate, but during the seventeenth century, up to around 1675, rims became much broader and flatter, their width approaching almost a quarter of the diameter of the plate. These were gradually succeeded by narrower rims with reeded mouldings, the earliest being incised into the upper edge of the rim; but raised mouldings were soon being cast as an integral part of the plate itself. Triple-reeded designs flourished *c*. 1670–90, after which they were replaced by single reeds. Where decoration was required, it was executed either with a graver, with punches, or in the form of wriggled-work, in which fine zig-zag lines were incised into the metal by rocking a narrow chisel-shaped blade across its surface. Floral designs using this method were particularly popular from the mid-late seventeenth century.

There are references to silver trenchers as early as 1521, but it is probable that they were for use at the after-dinner banquet course of sweetmeats, rather than at the dinner or supper table proper. Later inventories, such as that of Thomas Lord Wharton of Healaugh of 1568, list items such as '26 playtes parcell gilt with the bulls head [his crest] upon the same 9 score 4 unces at 4s. 8d. le unce £42.18.8d'. Each plate therefore weighed seven ounces, and perhaps measured eight inches or less in diameter. The use of silver dinner-plates appears to have become much more widespread on the fashionable table after the Restoration of Charles II. In 1670, for example, Prince Rupert bought sixty silver plates from Alderman Backwell, while in 1686 Prince George of Denmark purchased two dozen 17¾ oz. plates and the same number of 21 oz. trenchers from Child and Rogers. Very few plates of this date have survived through to the present day, but examples are known from the family plate of the Earls of Bathurst, 1686, and Lord St Oswald, 1686.[21]

The use of pottery dinner plates was virtually unknown in sixteenth-century England, but it was in this period that the necessary skills and knowledge which would eventually lead to their manufacture were introduced into this country by Jasper Andries and Jacob Jansen of

Antwerp. These refugees from the bloody activities of the Spanish Inquisition in the Low Countries arrived in Norwich by 1567, setting up a pottery there 'for the makeing of Galley pavinge tyles and Vessels for potycaries', which operated up to the end of the seventeenth century. The *galleywares*, better known today as delftware, were made of a pale buff-firing earthenware coated in a glossy lead glaze rendered an opaque white by the addition of tin oxide. It presented an extremely clean and bright appearance, especially when painted with metallic oxides before the glaze was fired to give vivid polychrome effects.

By 1571, a further pottery had been set up in Duke's Place, Aldgate, London, where work was carried on until *c.* 1615. Here, in addition to making tiles and ointment pots, they made dishes and chargers almost identical to those they had been making in Antwerp. The earliest dated example is a small charger some ten inches in diameter, its centre being painted with a view of a major fortification, probably the nearby Tower of London, with the inscription '*The rose is red the leaves are grene God save Elizabeth our Queene/1600*'. Around the rim, meanwhile, runs an Italianate border, in dark blue and yellow ochre, perhaps reflecting the Italian ancestry of Aldgate's Flemish potters. The success of these wares was reflected in the proliferation of further delftware potteries in Southwark (including Montagu Close *c.* 1613; Pickleherring, by 1618; Rotherhithe, 1638; Still Stairs, 1663; Bear Garden, 1671; and Gravel Lane, 1694); Lambeth (Copthall, 1676; Norfolk House, 1680; Vauxhall, 1683); and at the Hermitage, Wapping, from *c.* 1665. In addition, an offshoot of the Southwark potteries was founded at Brislington near Bristol about 1650, and at the Temple, Bristol, in 1683.

There is little evidence to show that the smaller chargers made at these potteries in the early seventeenth century were used for dining, their concave bodies and relatively

small foot-rings making them unsuitable for that purpose. By *c.* 1625–30, however, plates with flat bases and flat rims, similar to those of contemporary pewter-ware, and measuring some seven inches in diameter were being made in Southwark, their blue and blue-wash brushwork inspired by the designs on imported Ming porcelains. Chinoiserie continued to provide a constant source of inspiration for the delftware potters through into the eighteenth century; other devices included armorials, royal portraits, and short pithy inscriptions exhibiting a beautiful, free calligraphy, such as 'You & i are Earth, 1661'.[22]

14.
Delftware
These delftware plates, decorated in cobalt blue on a white ground, were all made in London potteries, (A) dating from the mid-seventeenth century, (B) from 1661, and (C) from the last quarter of the century.

Once the table had been laid in a Tudor nobleman's **Serving**
dining chamber, the Gentleman Usher confirmed that the
meal was ready before proceeding to knock at the door of
his master's lodgings, and conducting him to the table. In
the meantime, the chief cook had set out the dishes in
their correct order on the dresser at the service end of the
hall. On the Gentleman Usher's command, the Sewer
then went from the dining chamber, down through the
hall, where the Usher of the Hall cried 'Gentlemen and
yeoman wait upon the Sewer for my Lord!', and at least six
men then joined the Sewer at the dresser. As the Sewer's
procession returned to the hall screen, the Usher of the
Hall then cried 'By your leave my masters!', before leading
them through the hall, those present all standing
bareheaded while they passed by. At the dining chamber
door the Gentleman Usher ushered them to the table, and
ensured that the dishes were laid in the correct position.
Any meat which had to be carved was taken to a side-table
by the Carver, the carved meat required at the lord's table
being served next, and the Gentlemen of the Chamber
acting as waiters throughout the meal. The identical
procedure was followed for the service of the second
course. After the service was completed in the dining
chamber, the Carver supervised the clearing of the table;
and the voider containing the used bread trenchers was
removed by a yeoman usher. The meat was taken down
into the hall, where it was distributed by the Sewer, with
the advice of the Gentleman Usher, to the remainder of
the household.[23]

At the royal table, the ceremonial was much grander,
especially for state occasions. On December 27th, 1584,
Lupold von Wedel, a German visitor, observed Elizabeth
dine in state after her return from a Christmas service in
her chapel:

> While she was in church, a long table was made
> ready [on a dais] under a canopy of cloth of

gold. On her return from Church there were
served at this table forty large and silver dishes,
all of gilt silver, with various meats. She alone
took her seat at table . . . A young gentleman
habited in black carved the meats for the Queen
and a gentleman of about the same age arrayed
in green served her beverages. This gentleman had
to remain kneeling as long as she was drinking;
when she had finished, he rose and removed the
goblet. At the table, to her right stood gentlemen
of rank . . . white staffs in their hands [the
symbols of their high rank as household officers].

When the queen summoned one of them, he kneeled
until commanded to rise, bowed, went to the centre of the
room and bowed again, then ordered the sewers to bring
the next course, which was preceded by four gentlemen
with sceptres.[24] Normally the queen dined in great
privacy, but even so a high degree of ceremonial was
maintained when the dishes were placed on an empty
table outside her inner chamber. After the cloth had been
laid there came two gentlemen, one with a rod and the
other with a salt-cellar, a plate and bread:

when they had kneeled, and placed what was
brought upon the table, they retired [after
kneeling once more]. At last came an unmarried
lady (we were told she was a countess) and along
with her a married one, bearing a tasting knife;
the former dressed in white silk, who, when she
had prostrated herself three times, in the most
graceful manner, approached the table, and
rubbed the plates with the bread and salt, with as
much care as if the Queen had been present:
when they had waited there a little time, the
yeomen of the guard entered bareheaded,
cloathed in scarlet with a gold rose upon their
backs, bringing in at each turn, a course of four

and twenty dishes, served in plate, most of it gilt;
these dishes were received by a gentleman in the
same order, they were brought and placed upon
the table, while the lady taster gave to each of the
guard a mouthful to eat, for fear of poison.
During the time that this guard, which consists of
the tallest and stoutest men that can be found in
all England, being carefully selected for this
service, were bringing dinner, twelve trumpets,
and two kettle-drums made the hall ring for half
an hour together. At the end of all this
ceremonial, a number of unmarried ladies
appeared, who with particular solemnity lifted the
meats off the table, and conveyed it into the
Queen's inner and more private chamber, where,
after she had chosen for herself, the rest goes to
the ladies of the court. The Queen sups and dines
alone with very few attendants, and it is very
seldom that any body, foreigner or native, is
admitted at that time, and then only at the
intercession of somebody in power.[25]

In complete contrast, James I enjoyed dining in public.
When Sir Henry Wooten visited him in Scotland in 1601,
he noted that:

Anyone may enter the King's presence while he is
at dinner, and as he eats he converses with those
about him ... Dinner finished, he remains at
table for a time before he retires, listening to
banter and merry jests in which he takes great
delight.[26]

Even so, the ceremonial service of food continued to
provide an important visual reinforcement of the concept
of the power and prestige of monarchy.

Chargers and dishes

The large chargers and dishes upon which the food was carried from the kitchens and laid upon the table were of metal in the Tudor period, pewter being by far the most usual, although gold, silver gilt or silver were used by royalty and perhaps by some of the highest nobility. Their decoration, if any, could comprise stamped motifs, or an engraved armorial or initials, but the finest were given rich, florid line decoration cut with a graver or executed in wriggled-work during the mid-late seventeenth century. One example displaying the royal arms amid flowing mantling was inscribed *'Vivat Rex Carolus Secundus Beati Pacifi* 1662' to celebrate the restoration of Charles II, while naïve horses could be accompanied with the singularly inappropriate lines of: *'When this yov see remember mee/EP. 1661'*[27]

From the late sixteenth century, the London delftware potters had been producing chargers with brightly

15.
Pewter Charger
The broad, flat surface of this large charger is almost entirely covered with finely engraved decoration featuring the Royal arms and portraits of Charles II and Catherine of Braganza. It probably dates from the 1660s.

coloured decoration executed in bold brushwork across their wide expanses of milk-white glaze. The best known of these were the 'blue-dash' chargers which took their name from the diagonal blue brush-strokes which gave an almost rope-like appearance to their rounded rims. Popular subjects painted on their faces included reigning monarchs, heroes such as the Duke of Marlborough or General Monk, biblical themes, especially Adam and Eve with the Tree of Knowledge and the serpent, or commemorative devices, such as the chargers made in 1680–81 concerning the ill-use of Siamese Twins from Somerset by two of the local gentry. Floral designs were also made in quantity, ranging from crude versions of the Netherlandish pomegranates and oranges to symmetrical sprays of tulips probably influenced by Turkish wares. Chargers of far higher quality might copy their designs from contemporary Continental engravings, from the Ming, Wan-Li, or K'ang Hsi porcelains of China, or from the Fécondité dishes made in mid-sixteenth-century France by Bernard Palissy. The latter were usually oval, a border incorporating a number of shallow concave wells decorated with Ming artemisia leaves, Renaissance masks, Dutch landscapes and perhaps the arms of the City Livery Companies enclosing a polychrome relief panel showing a naked woman surrounded by naked children. Plates of this type were chiefly made for decoration, frequently having two holes pierced through their foot-rims to enable them to be hung against a wall. The majority of delftware chargers were ideal for practical use, however, their broad concave bowls and easily cleaned glazes being perfectly suited for the service of food.

Delftware was not the only pottery technique to be brought into this country during this period. Slipware, a method of decorating lead-glazed earthenware by piping a thin solution of liquid clay (slip) onto unfired vessels through a goose-quill mounted on the tip of a bored-out cow's horn, was introduced into England from the Low

16.

Delftware Chargers
The upper charger, the earlist dated English example, was made in 1660 at the Aldgate pottery of Jasper Andries and Jacob Jansen, immigrant potters from Antwerp. Its decoration is carried out in brightly-coloured metallic oxides which were painted on the glaze before its final firing. The lower example was probably made at the Pickleherring pottery at Southwark in 1635. The scene is taken from an engraving by Crispin de Passe (1564–1637) after a painting by John Overbeck. The initials probably refer to Thomas Townsend and his wife Maria, daughter of the potter Christian Wilhelm.

17.
The chargers made by the English earthenware potters from the mid seventeenth century were decorated with liquid clay called slip. The upper charger was made by Thomas Toft of Stoke-on-Trent, probably in the 1670s using slip-trailing, a method by which coloured slips were piped on to the charger through a goose-quill nozzle fitted to the bored-out tip of a cow horn. Its theme is Charles II hiding in the Boscobel oak. In contrast, the lower charger made in red-brown clay was dipped in a white slip, which was then scraped away to produce a floral pattern. Made in North Devon *c.* 1650–75, it is a fine example of the sgraffito wares tyical of this region.

Countries in the late 16th – early 17th centuries. This gave the native potters an extremely rapid, simple and versatile decorative technique which enabled them to produce more attractive wares for use on the dining table. By 1612 potters at Wrotham in Kent were making wares of this type, as were the Essex potteries which served the London market. The 'Metropolitan' wares of Essex, with their red clays decorated with concentric designs of scrolled fleur-de-lis, leaves, and roses etc., in white slip appear to have been carried up the east coast, perhaps as return cargoes for the Newcastle collier vessels. They were then taken inland to be copied at the local potteries. As a result of new marketing techniques adopted by the north country pottery trade in the mid-seventeenth century, the potters of Staffordshire were enabled to exploit their unique range of clays, a plentiful supply of coal, and their cheap foodstuffs to make Staffordshire the predominant area for ceramic production in England, a position it has maintained ever since. A number of potters in the Stoke-on-Trent area now began to make slipware chargers of superlative quality, of which those by Thomas Toft were the finest. Measuring some 18 inches or more in diameter, their faces bore colourful illustrations of the monarchy, including Charles in the Boscobel oak, the King and Queen, the Royal arms, as well as popular themes ranging from Adam and Eve to mermaids.[28]

While slip-trailing dominated the English eastern and northern earthenware potter's art from the early seventeenth century, a different tradition had been established in the West Country. Here the *sgraffito* technique was used, in which red-firing clay vessels were dipped in an overall white slip which, when dry, was scratched away to reveal the darker clay beneath, the whole then being coated in a golden yellow lead glaze. It had its beginnings in the first half of the sixteenth century, and flourished as a method of decorating chargers from the early to mid-seventeenth century, when simple concentric compositions of lines and dots or compass-work began to be used. Later in the century they were replaced by lively depictions of cockerels and tulips, female figures, birds and floral compositions. The main centres of production were at Donyatt in Somerset and the coastal area of North Devon. The slipwares and sgraffito wares made by seventeenth-century English potteries are unlikely to have been used on the dining tables of the upper sections of society, even though Samuel Pepys recorded in his diary for September 6th, 1666, that he had 'dined on an earthen platter'. Instead, they probably served on the tables of the small gentry and lesser merchants, acting as a substitute for the finer delftwares.[29]

The dishes of food were not placed on the table in a haphazard manner but, as with every aspect of formal dining, skilfully arranged for the convenience of the diners. Perhaps the most detailed description of this process is given by Gervase Markham:[30] **The arrangement of the dishes**

> what availes it our good *House-wife* to bee never
> so skilfull in the parts of cookery, if she want skill
> to marshall the dishes, and set everyone in his
> due place, giving precedency according to fashion
> and custome ... It is then to be understood that
> it is the office of the Clerke of the Kitchen
> (whose place our *House-wife* must many times
> supply) to order the meate at the Dresser, and
> deliver it to the sewer, who is to deliver it to the
> Gentlemen and Yeomen-waiters to beare to the
> table ... She shall first marshall her sallets,
> delivering the grand sallet first, which is evermore
> compound: then greene sallets, then boyld sallets,
> then some smaller compound sallets. Next unto
> sallets she shall deliver foorth all her fricases, the
> simple first, as collops, rashers, and such like;
> then compound fricases, after them all her boyld

meats in their degree, as simple broths, stewed broth, and the boylings of sundry fowles. Next them all sorts of rost meates, of which the greatest first, as chine of Beefe, or surloyne, the gigget or Legges of Mutton, Goose, Swan, Veale, Pig, Capon and such like. Then bak't meates, the hot first, as Fallow-deere in Pastry . . . Then cold bak't meates, Pheasant, Partridges . . . Then lastly Carbonados both simple and compound. And thus being marshald from the Dresser, the Sewer upon placing them on the table, shall not set them down as he receive them, but setting the sallets extravagantly about the table, mixe the Fricases aboute them, then the boild meates among the Fricases, rost meates amongst the boild, bak't meates amongst the rost, and Carbonados among the bak't; so that before every trencher stand a Sallet a Fricase, a Boild meate, a Rost meate, a Bak't meat, and a Carbonado, which will give a most comely beauty to the table, and very great contentment to the Guests.

So likewise in the second course she shall first preferre the lesser wild-fowle . . . then the lesser land-fowle . . . Then the greater land-fowle . . . Then hot bak't meates . . . Then cold bak't meates, and these also shall be marshald at the Table, as the first course, not one kind all together . . . and Quelquechoses [Kickshaws] which relie on the invention of the Cooke, they are to be thrust in into every place that is emptie, and so sprinkled over all the table: and this is the best method for the extraordinary great feasts of Princes.

This account might give the impression that the dishes were scattered across the table, but in fact they were set

A Table for 38 Perſons, coverd with 43 Diſhes & 24 Hors-d' œuvres.

Tab:39

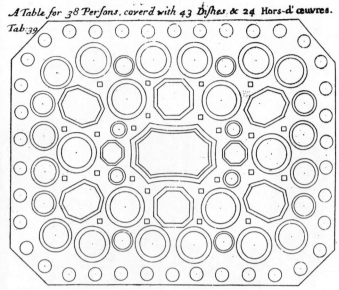

18.
Table Plan
The symmetrical arrangement of dishes on the dining table is clearly illustrated in this plan published in Patrick Lamb's *Royal Cookery; or The Complete Court-Cook* of 1710.

down in precise symmetrical patterns. Evidence for this is provided by contemporary illustrations, such as the National Portrait Gallery's *Life and Death of Sir Henry Unton* of *c.* 1596, in which twelve diners sit around a long rectangular table. Five (or perhaps six) large dishes are spaced out down the centre of the table, with a row of six smaller side dishes aranged in a parallel row down each side, the outer edges of the table being occupied by the diners' square-cut trenchers. Similar formal designs were probably used throughout the seventeenth century, some of the most magnificent being those designed by Patrick Lamb, for fifty years the Master Cooke to Charles II, James II, William and Mary, and Queene Anne. His *Royal-Cookery* published posthumously in 1710 included detailed table plans for coronation dinners, wedding suppers, royal dinners and feasts, with the positions of anything up to 114 dishes and 83 hors d'oeuvres precisely indicated. Similar schemes were followed on the tables at

19.
Table Setting
Using a variety of
sources of
information, including
furniture style, cutlery,
recipe books, etc., it is
possible to re-create
the appearance of a
typical late
seventeenth century
dinner table with a
high degree of
accuracy.

every level of polite society, even when only five or nine
dishes appeared at each course.

In order to permit the most economical use of the table-
space, and to display the major dishes to best effect, dish-
rings were introduced in the last quarter of the
seventeenth century. Randle Holme's *Academy of
Armoury* of 1688 describes these accessories as circular,
hexagonal or octagonal stands, the top and bottom being
identical so that they could be used either way up, their

20.
Dish Ring
The dish ring was developed in the late seventeenth century to enable dishes of food to be elevated above the level of the table, making an impresive display, in addition to saving valuable space. This particular example was made by Samual Hood in London in 1697.

purpose being to 'make the feast look full and noble'. Surviving examples date from around 1685, their workmanship and decoration usually being of the highest quality.

Garnishing

The formality of the table-setting was extended to include the arrangement of food on the serving dish from the late sixteenth century at least. Before this time most roast meats were served with little or no garnish, while stewed meats were served on a bed of crustless cubes of bread called sops or sippets, which absorbed the juices and enabled them to be easily scooped up with a spoon. In his *Good Huswife's Jewell* of 1596, however, Thomas Dawson was advising his readers to arrange prunes, yellow barberries (from the Berberis shrub), fruit or hard-boiled eggs around the rim of the dish, while in 1615 John Murrell advised the cook:

> Garnish your Dishes round about with fine
> Sugar: take Orangado dipt among Biskets and
> Carrawaies. Take a Pomegranate, and garnish the
> side of your Dish with it, take Currins, and
> Prunes, and wrap them in fine Sugar, having
> beene first boyled tender in faire water. Take a
> Lemmon and slice it, and put it on your Dish,
> and large Mace steeped or boyled, or preserved
> Barberryes. Any of these are fit to garnish your
> Dish: take your Capon out of the broth, and put

it into a Dish with sippets, and any of these
garnishes round about it.[31]

Other garnishes might include kidneys, the bottoms of
artichokes, sweetbreads, or grapes as described in de La
Varenne's *The French Cook* of 1653, or the oysters, pickles,
mushrooms, horseradish, etc., that were listed in other
contemporary sources.[32]

Sippets tended to go out of use in the late seventeenth
century, their demise being a direct result of the
introduction of dining forks; but the formal arrangement
of foods had by now found its greatest potential in the
salad dishes which had been growing in popularity since
the Elizabethan period. It reached its most extreme form
in the grand salad, the first dish carried to the table. *The
Second Book of Cookery* (in the fifth edition of 1638) for
example, describes how to set out a green salad of
shredded lettuce and herbs with almonds, dried and fresh
fruits. Firstly five half-lemons stuck with branches of
rosemary hung with cherries were arranged cross-wise in
the bed of the salad, interspersed with four halved hard-
boiled eggs stuck with sliced almonds and dates. A border
of alternating quartered eggs and slices of lemon was then
arranged within the brim of the dish, the rim itself being
garnished with orange segments and small piles of capers
to produce a particularly rich and colourful appearance.
Later in the seventeenth century chopped cold meats,
boiled eggs, pickles and shellfish of contrasting colours
were heaped in segmental patterns on an upturned dish
standing within a larger bowl, their junctions and borders
being garnished with further anchovies or pickles, to
produce a 'Solomon Gundy', the anglicised form of the
French *salmigondis*. Dishes such as these, together with
great decorated and glazed pasties, open-topped pies
garnished either with fried rolled sage-leaves and meat
balls, or with separately baked lids elaborately pierced and
built up in interlacing strips, all contributed to the

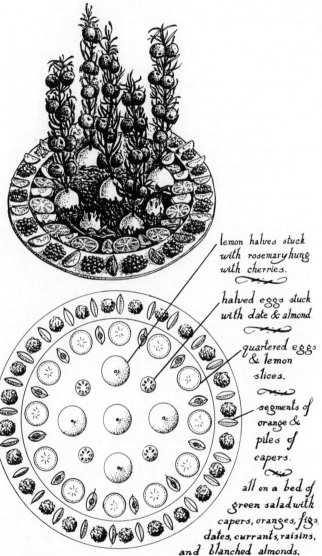

21.
Garnishing
The grand salad, the first in the procession of dishes carried up through the hall to the dining chamber, provides a good example of the colourful and symmetrical garnishing typical of the late Tudor and earlier Stuart periods.

lemon halves stuck with rosemary hung with cherries.

halved eggs stuck with date & almond.

quartered eggs & lemon slices.

segments of orange & piles of capers.

all on a bed of green salad with capers, oranges, figs, dates, currants, raisins, and blanched almonds.

magnificent display of richness and colour which characterised the dining tables of Stuart England.

The ewery Washing the hands before and after dining was an extremely important social custom during the mediaeval period when fingers were used to hold meat as it was being carved, and to carry food from the trencher to the mouth. For this purpose, a cupboard or ewery standing at one side of the dining parlour was equipped with all the necessary utensils: the *Book of Kervinge* directs that 'thyn ewery be arayed with basyns and ewers and water hote and colde'.

To start the full mediaeval ceremony, the surnap, a long towel, was laid over the tablecloth. To do this, the Sewer held one end of the surnap at one end of the table, the Gentleman Usher fastening his rod in it in order to draw it down the full length of the table bowing to the sovereign as he passed. Kneeling down, the Sewer and Gentleman Usher stretched the cloth, the Usher then proceeding to a point opposite one side of his sovereign where he bowed before using his rod to raise a fold perhaps half a yard wide across the surnap to produce an 'estate'. He then repeated this process on the other side of the sovereign before returning to kneel at his end of the table once more to straighten the surnap without removing the estates. Now the surnap was in place, the Gentleman Usher stood directly in front of his sovereign, rod in hand, bowed, and returned to his end of the table while the sovereign washed his hands. Then, the Gentlemen Usher used his rod to lift up his end of the surnap and carry it to the centre of the table, the Sewer bringing his end up to the same point before carrying the surnap back to its place at the ewery.[33]

On state occasions, this ceremony was lavish in the extreme. Lupold von Wedel recorded how Elizabeth I: 'rose and turned her back upon the table, whereupon two bishops stepped forward and said grace. After them came three earls . . . These three took a large basin, which was

22.
Ewer and Basin
Used to wash the hands before and after dining, this magnificent ewer and its basin were made in silver gilt in 1617, and form part of the civic plate of the city of Norwich.

covered like a meat dish and of gilt silver and two of the older gentlemen held the towel. The five of them then advanced to the Queen and knelt down before her. They then raised the lid from the basin . . . The third poured water over the Queen's hands, who before washing her hands drew off a ring and handed it to the Lord Chamberlain. After washing her hands she again drew on the ring.[34]

The ewers used to pour the water, and the matching basins which caught the falling drops, were among the most lavish pieces of domestic plate, frequently being of silver gilt worked in the most elegant and ornate manner. The broad-rimmed basins had the centres of their deep,

concave bowls raised up as a boss which, in addition to
providing a focal point for the display of armorials, etc.,
could offer a pedestal for the ewer when the pieces were
displayed on the ewery or sideboard. Such examples are
found as late as the reign of Charles I, after which plainer
fashion prevails, the salver being quite unornamented,
and the ewers somewhat plain jugs, with or without stems,
and with simple handles. With the accession of James II
the inverted helmet shape was introduced, this form
continuing through to the mid-eighteenth century. By
this time the ewers and basins had passed out of all
practical use, since the widespread use of dining forks in
the mid-seventeenth century meant that diners kept their
fingers clean throughout the meal.

With the second washing of the hands, the meal came
to an end in the dining chamber, or dining parlour, but
from the mid-sixteenth century onwards for an
entertainment of any quality, the best was yet to come. In
a separate room, perhaps on the leads of the roof, or in an
elevated corner of the garden, an ambrosial third course
or 'banquet' of fruit, sweetmeats and sweet spiced wines
awaited, their colour, perfume, modelling and table
settings being even more luxurious than those of dinner
itself. Here all formality disappeared, and an exceedingly
good time was had by the select few invited to attend.[35]

Notes and References

1. Sir H. Cholmley, *Memoirs* (London, 1787) p.56.
2. D. Parsons, *The Diary of Sir Henry Slingsby of Scriven* (London, 1836) pp.24–5.
3. Sir W. H. St. J. Hope, *Cowdray and Easebourne Priory* (London, 1919) p.128.
4. R. Warner, *Antiquitates Culinariae* (London, 1791) p.xlv.
5. *A Collection of Ordinances & Regulations for the Government of the Royal Household made in Diverse Reigns* (London, 1790) p.370.
6. Warner, p.li.
7. L. G. Matthews & H. J. M. Green, 'Post-Medieval Pottery of the Inns of Court' *Post-Medieval Archaeology* 3 (1969) p.16; B. Bloice, 'Norfolk House, Lambeth . . .' *Post-Medieval Archaeology* 5 (1971) p.126.

8. *A Perfect School of Instructions for the Officers of the Mouth* (London, 1682) pp.110–24.
9. *The Babees Book (1475)*, ed. F. J. Furnivall (Early English Text Society, OS 32, 1868) lines 143–5.
10. P. Brears, *Yorkshire Probate Inventories 1542–1689* (Leeds, 1972) p.29.
11. J. F. Hayward, *English Cutlery* (London, 1957) p.2.
12. For these and similar references, see *Oxford English Dictionary*, 'Forks'.
13. B. Jonson, *Volpone or the Fox* (1607) Act IV Scene 1.
14. Quoted in Warner, pp.liii–iv.
15. Ibid., p.134.
16. W. Caxton, *Eneydos 1490*, ed. W. T. Culley and F. J. Furnivall (Early English Text Society, ES 57, 1890) pp.121–2; C. A. Wilson, *Food and Drink in Britain* (Harmondsworth, 1984) p.219.
17. *Northumberland Household Book; the Regulations and Establishment of the Household of Henry Algernon Percy . . . 1512* (London, 1905) pp.xv,73; 75; 78; F. G. Emmison, *Tudor Food and Pastimes* (London, 1964) p.91.
18. See *Oxford English Dictionary*, 'Trenchers'.
19. Warner, p.liii.
20. R.F. Michaelis, *Antique Pewter of the British Isles* (London, 1955) pp.14–26.
21. Brears (1972), p.29. W. J. Cripps, *Old English Plate* (London, 1891) pp.309–11.
22. For details of the early English delftwares, see F. Britton, *London Delftware* (London, 1987).
23. Hope, pp.125–6.
24. Quoted in M. Lorwin, *Dining with William Shakespeare* (New York, 1976) p.188.
25. Warner, p.xlv.
26. Lorwin, p.190.
27. H. H. Cotterell, *Old Pewter, its Makers & Marks* (London, 1929) pp.120–1.
28. P. Brears, *The English Country Pottery* (Newton Abbot, 1971); L. Weatherill, *The Pottery Trade & North Staffordshire 1660–1760* (Manchester, 1971).
29. R. Coleman-Smith & T. Pearson, *Excavations in the Donyatt Potteries* (Chichester, 1988); A. Grant, *North Devon Pottery: The Seventeenth Century* (Exeter, 1983).
30. G. Markham, *The English Hus-wife*, 4th ed. (London, 1631) p.137.
31. J. Murrell, *A New Booke of Cookerie* (London, 1615) p.54.
32. P. Brears, *The Gentlewoman's Kitchen* (Wakefield, 1984) pp.30–31.
33. *A Collection of Ordinances . . . . 1790*, p.119.
34. Lorwin, p.190.
35. C. A. Wilson, ed., *'Banquetting Stuffe': the Fare and Social Background of the Tudor and Stuart Banquet* (Edinburgh, 1989).

5.

Ideal Meals and their Menus from the Middle Ages to the Georgian Era

C. ANNE WILSON

Ideal meals are meals without a history. The menu was drawn up and written down, and in its time it existed as a visual reminder for both the host and the cook when they were choosing the fare for a specific meal in the near future. Some of these menus survive from the late fourteenth century onwards, but we do not know whether they were followed slavishly and repeatedly on many occasions, or whether they merely served as *aides mémoires* from which the cook took a few dishes, while adding others according to the raw materials he or she had to hand. We do know that the ideal menus of each period reflect the tastes of the times, and include many individual named dishes which are also to be found both on the menus of actual recorded feasts, and in recipe form in the cookery-books.

Such menus have their parameters. From the fourteenth to the seventeenth century alternative menus were drawn up for flesh days and fish days (by the seventeenth century often only one fasting-day menu among several fleshmeat menus). The seasons also placed limitations on the kinds of foods available, leading eventually to month by month menus. The following examples show how the genre of ideal menus developed and led to the documentation and illustration of table settings in eighteenth-century cookery-books.

Ideal Meals and their Menus

The earliest ideal menus to have come to light so far are those appended to two copies of the *Forme of Cury* made probably in the late fourteenth century not long after that famous cookery-book was compiled (very possibly, as a later copyist states, by the master cooks of King Richard II). The group comprises seven separate menus, five for fleshdays and two for fishdays. Three of the fleshday menus are further qualified (in short Latin headings) as being for 'around Michaelmas', 'at Eastertime' and 'at Pentecost'. Each menu is laid out in three courses, which suggests food to be prepared for important feasts; everyday meals and even some feasts were in two courses.

One of the two menus for an ordinary fleshday runs:

1st course
Boars' heads enarmed [larded], bruet of Almayne to pottage*, therewith teals baked & woodcocks, pheasants & curlews.

2nd course
Partridge, coneys, & malard, therewith *blanc desire**, caudel ferre* with flampoyntes of cream* & tarts.

3rd course
plovers, laverocks, & chickens farced [stuffed], and therewith *mawmeny**[1]

Glossary

*Bruet of Almayne: coneys or kids cut into small pieces, parboiled, reboiled with almond milk, rice-flour and spices, coloured red with alkanet, *Forme of Cury*, no. 48.
**Blanc desire:* thick sweet pottage of ground almonds and white wine (or almond milk) with rice-flour, ground chicken-flesh and sugar, *Forme of Cury*, no. 39.
*caudel ferre: wine sweetened, thickened with fine flour and heated with beaten egg-yolks, *Forme of Cury*, no. 43.
*flampoyntes of cream: open tarts with a creamy filling with pastry 'points' set in it, cf. *Forme of Cury*, nos. 116 and 192, with different fillings.
**mawmeny:* thick pottage of shredded chicken-flesh, rice-flour, sugar, wine, dates, pine-nuts and spices, coloured red with sandalwood: *Forme of Cury*, no. 22; and no. 202 for yellow version, with saffron.

There are signs that the ideal meal was being viewed in a more seasonal fashion, for monthly menus had begun to appear. *The Noble boke off cookry ffor a prynce householde or eny other estately houssolde* (the Holkham MS) begins with the menus of some notable feasts, including those for the coronation of King Henry V and for the Installation of Archbishop Neville in 1467.[2] But at the end of this section come menus headed 'Servys in the monthe of Januar' and 'Servys in the monthe of Fevrielle'. The menus then break off, and the cookery recipes begin.

For 'Fevrielle' the dishes are:

Brawn and mustard	Wigeons
Gruel [oatmeal pottage]	Partridges
Beef	Quails
Pestles [legs] of pork	Tansy
Swan	Fritter
Lamb	—
Heron	Wafers and hippocras (sweet spiced wine)

The social arrangements of the period are reflected in three menus from British Library MS Sloane 442.[3] The first two are for fleshday meals for the knights' table and the king's table respectively; the third is for a fishday meal for the king's table. The king's (or great lord's) table was the principal table in the Great Chamber, where most of the formal entertaining of the nobility took place. The knights' table was for guests whose estate was too low to permit them to sit at the principal table, but too high for them to dine with the steward and the rest of the household in the Hall.

At a superficial glance, the fleshday menus appear to be examples of a new genre: the ideal meal for the two tables of the Great Chamber. But the headings are misleading; for further research has revealed that both are derived from one actual feast, said to have been given for King Richard II and the Duke of Lancaster at the Bishop of Durham's palace in London on 23rd September 1387. The menu for that feast, which precedes the collection of cookery recipes in British Library MS Harleian 4016, was published in T. Austin's *Two Fifteenth-century Cookery-*

books.[4] The same dishes that are listed there reappear in
MS Sloane, 442, where they have been divided up
between the two tables in a rather curious way, for
although several of them are duplicated in each of the
menus, and although the king's table receives a greater
total number of dishes, the knights' table alone has been
assigned some of the more spectacular confections – the
custard Lumbard, the chickens endored, and also one
entirely new item not mentioned in the Harleian MS
(though it may of course have survived intact in other
copies of the menu of King Richard's feast): a roast
peacock. We can only speculate as to whether the 'ideal'
menus thus created were ever put to practical use in the
Great Chambers of the nobility and, if so, whether the
speciality dishes were reassigned to the principal table.

A quite different fifteenth-century ideal meal is the
feast for a franklin proposed by John Russell in his *Boke of
Nurture* of around 1450.[5] The estate of a franklin was just
below the lesser gentry and just above the yeomen
farmers. It is possible that his family might have possessed
a manuscript medical recipe book at this period, but most
unlikely that they would have kept written copies either of
cookery recipes or of menus: such information would
have been passed on orally. John Russell's suggestions for
a celebratory meal may owe something to his personal
experience of the hospitality of franklins.

Russell himself claimed to have been in the service of
Humphrey, Duke of Gloucester, which may account for
his reference to Chamber and Hall. The franklin's house
might not have been grand enough to contain either
room, but he would have had a privy parlour in which to
entertain his friends, while the servants and labourers ate
in the all-purpose living-room-cum-kitchen. Here is his
feast (the spelling has been modernised):

> A Franklin may make a feast improberabille,*
> Brawn with mustard is concordable,
>   bacon served with peason [peas]

Beef or mutton stewed serviceable,
Boiled chicken or capon agreeable,
　　convenient for the season;
Roasted goose & pig full profitable
Capon bakemeat or custard*, costable
　　when eggs and cream be geson [scarce].
Therefore stuff of household is behovable,
Mortrews* or jussel* are delectable
　　for the second course by reason.
The veal, lamb, kid or cony,
Chicken or pigeon roasted tenderly,
　　bakemeats or dowsets* with all.
Then following, fritters & a leach* lovely;
Such service in season is full seemly
　　to serve with both chamber & hall.
Then apples & pears with spices delicately
After the time of the year full daintily
　　with bread and cheese to call,
Spiced cakes and wafers worthily
With bragot* & mead, thus men may merrily
　　please well both great & small.

Glossary

improberabille: a made-up word, probably intended to mean
　　'irreproachable'.
custard: a baked savoury custard tart, with pieces of cooked
　　meat, small birds, etc. set in the filling.
mortrews: a pottage of ground-up chicken, pork or fish, with
　　almond milk, spices, etc., thickened with rice-flour.
jussel: meat broth thickened with eggs or breadcrumbs.
dowsets: small, sweet custard tarts.
leach: a sweet, solid confection made from curds or from
　　honey and breadcrumbs, with dates, spices, etc., and
　　served out in slices.
bragot: ale sweetened with honey.

The sixteenth century In 1500 the printer Richard Pynson produced the first English printed cookery-book from a manuscript containing many of the same recipes as the Holkham MS. It began with a similar claim to be a book for the household of a prince or a person of high estate.

But around the middle of the century a new kind of cookery-book appeared. *A Proper Newe Booke of Cokerye*, was printed several times (copies from the 1570s survive), and was intended for the families of the new merchant classes who were coming up in the world.[6] The ideal menus at the beginning of the book were subsequently pirated by the unknown 'A.W.' who compiled *A Booke of Cookry Very Necessary to All such as Delight Therein* in 1584 (with later editions), so they continued to be issued as exemplars over a period of nearly fifty years.

A small two-course dinner and a two-course supper precede the following grand menu for 'The Service at Dinner' (note the seasonal adjustments for the geese and swan):

First Course
Brawn and mustard
Capons stewed, or in white broth
A pestle of venison upon brewes*
A chine of beef and a breast of mutton boiled
Chewets* or pies of fine mutton
Three green geese in a dish, sorrel sauce; for a stubble goose, mustard and vinegar. After All Haloween Day, a swan, sauce chawdron*
A pig
A double rib of beef roasted, sauce pepper and vinegar
A loin of veal or breast, sauce oranges
Half a lamb or a kid
Two capons roasted, sauce wine and salt, ale and salt, except it be upon sops*
Two pasties of fallow deer in a dish
A dish of leach*

Second Course
Jelly
Peacock, sauce wine and salt
Two coneys or half a dozen rabbits*, sauce mustard and sugar
Half a dozen chickens upon sorrel sops
Half a dozen pigeons

Mallard	
Teal	
Gulls	Sauce mustard and vinegar
Stork	
Heronsewe	
Crane	
Curlew	Sauce galentine*
Bittern	

Bustard
Pheasant, sauce water and salt with onions sliced
Half a dozen of woodcocks, sauce mustard and sugar
Half a dozen partridges
Half a dozen rails (birds), sauced as the pheasants
A dozen of quails
A dish of larks
A pasty of red deer
Tart
Gingerbread
Fritters

Glossary

brewes: sops of bread (see below).

chewets: small round pies, often fried rather than baked.

chawdron: sauce made with the swan's blood and entrails, and breadcrumbs.

sops: pieces of crustless bread or toast laid on the bottom of the dish under boiled meat.

leach: in the sixteenth century, a solid milk or almond milk jelly, cut into cubes or pieces of other shapes.

rabbits: in the sixteenth century, very young coneys.

galentine: sauce made with spices and breadcrumbs with wine or vinegar.

The seventeenth century In 1605 a new copy was made of the regulations for the household of the Marquis of Donegal. It included a month by month 'dietary'. Here under the name of each month appeared a long list of the food animals in season, with separate sections for quadrupeds; fowls, including a great number of wild birds; and fish. Next came a menu for dinner, followed by one for supper. January and alternate months to November were supplied with fleshmeat meals; February and the remaining months to December with fishday meals. This arrangement did not, of course, reflect the eating customs of the day. Fishdays occurred weekly on Fridays, and there were attempts to enforce them on Wednesdays and Saturdays too during the reigns of Queen Elizabeth and King James I, while

Lent was devoted entirely to fasting-day food. The ideal
menus in this book had to be adjusted for use according to
the day of the week, with borrowings made from the
menus of adjacent months as appropriate.

The food is varied but very simply prepared. There is no
advice about sauces here (the cooks of a great nobleman's
house were trained to know the correct sauces without
needing to consult a book; the book itself would have
been an aide-memoire for the Comptroller of the
Household, who would have passed on the general
instructions to the Clerk of the Kitchen; and he
instructed the cooks).

For July 1605 the following is 'A Diatree for Dinner':[7]

The second course

Lamb ro.	Godwits
Pheasant	Knots
Bittern	Quails
Rabbits	Peewits
Pigeons	Grouse
Chickens	Martins
Partridges	Larks
Pigeons baked	Tart
Dotterels	Red deer baked
Kennices*	

The first course

Capon boiled	Shoveler
Veal bo.	Venison ro.
Birds bo.	Gull ro.
Rabbits bo.	Egret ro.
Neat's tongue bo.	Brewe ro.
Lamb bo.	Custard
Beef roasted	Heron ro.
Veal ro.	Turkey
Pig ro.	Hare ro.
Minced pie	Capon
Green goose	Fallow deer
Stork	

Kennices: wild birds (possibly gannets).   **Glossary**

A fishday menu is described in John Murrell's *A New Booke of Cookerie*, published in 1617 (and later republished more than once in his *Two Books of Cookerie and Carving*: the fifth edition appeared in 1638). At the beginning are the menus for a summer feast of 50 dishes in three courses, a winter feast of 40 dishes in two courses, and 'a small common service' of 24 dishes in two courses. All list the fare for a fleshmeat day, but they are followed by a fasting-day menu. Here, as in all the other menus, each item is separately numbered, and in his introduction Murrell explained why: 'These directions serve both for a bill of fare, and to serve out your meats in good order.' The order in which dishes were carried into the room and laid upon the table was carefully worked out at this period, as is clear from Gervase Markham's detailed instructions for the serving in of a feast.[8]

Here is John Murrell's 'Bill of fare for fish-dayes, and Fasting-dayes, Ember-weekes, or Lent:[9]

The first course for the same dyet
1. A dish of butter
2. Rice milk
3. Buttered eggs
4. Stewed oysters
5. A boiled roach or gurnet
6. A boiled salad of herbs or of carrots
7. A boiled pike
8. Buttered loaves
9. Chewets of ling or stockfish
10. Another salad
11. Stewed trouts or smelts
12. A dish of buttered stockfish
13. Salt eel or white herring
14. A jowl [head & shoulders] of ling
15. A skirret-pie
16. Buttered flounders or plaice
17. An eel or carp pie
18. Haddock, fresh cod, or whiting
19. Salt salmon
20. A custard

The second course for this dyet
1. A boiled carp
2. Spitchcocks* of eels
3. Fried stockfish
4. Boiled eels
5. Baked puffs
6. A roasted eel
7. Buttered parsnips
8. Fried oysters
9. Blanced manchet in a fryingpan
10. A fried roach
11. An oyster pie
12. Fried smelts
13. A pippin pie
14. Fried flounders
15. Buttered crabs
16. Fried skirrets
17. A tart of spinach or of carrots
18. Conger
19. Lobster or prawns
20. Pickled oysters.

Spitchcock: an eel split and grilled.

Robert May favoured the month by month approach for the specimen menus at the beginning of his *The Accomplisht Cook*, published in 1665. His choice of headings for the first three rather conceals this arrangement: they are All Saints Day, Christmas Day and New Year's Day, representing November, December and January respectively. All are for feasts of the two courses of twenty dishes each variety. But the remaining nine menus are headed by the names of the months from February to October, and they are for more modest dinners with no more than six main dishes to each of the two courses. The food itself is plentiful, and the dishes would have served a number of people.

For the month of September, the menu offered in *The Accomplisht Cook*[10] was:

I	II
1. An olio*	1. Rabbits
2. Breast of veal in stoffado	2. Two hearns, one larded
3. Twelve partridges hashed	3. Florentine* of tongues
4. Grand salad	4. 8 pigeons roast, 4 larded
5. Chawdron* salad	5. Pheasant pouts*, 2 larded
6. Custard	6. A cold hare pie

Selsey cockles broiled [grilled] after

Glossary

olio: sliced-up meat and vegetables in a rich, spicy sauce, of Spanish origin.

chawdron: entrails.

florentine: tart containing finely chopped meat with spices, candied and dried fruits, and other delicacies.

pouts: young birds.

The eighteenth century: menus and table-settings

As the seventeenth century drew to a close, a new method was discovered for conveying the way to set out dishes upon the table to the readers of cookery-books. Folding-plate illustrations had rarely appeared in those books hitherto; but folding-plates showing table-settings seem to have been incorporated in F. Massialot's *Le Cuisinier Roial et Bourgeois* of 1691. They were soon copied in another French publication, Monsieur Audiger's *La Maison Reglée* of 1692, in which small folding-plates bear diagrams demonstrating the position of large, medium-sized and small dishes upon a properly served table. The table is oval, and on it are engraved circles inscribed with the word *plat,* which are positioned to show how each should be placed at a meal for six diners. At the centre is the largest circle called *grand plat,* flanked by two *moyens plats* on the long axis of the table and two *petits plats* on the shorter axis. Six still smaller empty circles around the periphery represent the *couvertures* for the diners (see Figure 23). There was a certain economy in this arrangement, since Audiger was able to explain in the accompanying text which foods were to appear in each course at the places occupied by the *plats*: at the first course, the *grand plat* was to be a *grand pottage,* and the

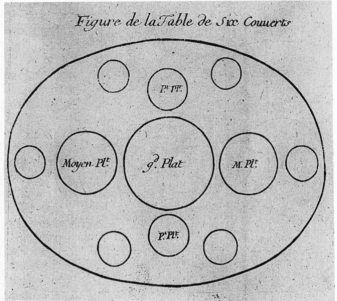

Figure de la Table de Six Couuerts

P.ᵗ Pl.ᵗ

Moyen Pl.ᵗ   g.ᵈ Plat   M. Pl.ᵗ

P.ᵗ Pl.ᵗ

23.
Early French table
diagram, showing
grand plat, moyens and
petits plats from M.
Audiger, *La Maison
Reglée*, 1692.

moyens plats two entrees; at the second course, the *grand plat* was to be a dish of roast meats, the *moyens plats* were to hold two salads, and the *petits plats* either *ragoûts* or *entremets*.

This new style of representing plates upon the table-top arrived in England with the publication in 1702 of *The Court and Country Cook*, an English translation which combined Massialot's *Cuisinier Roial et Bourgeois* with his *Nouvelles Instructions pour les Confitures* of 1692. In the illustrations to *The Court and Country Cook* the table itself is much more prominent than in Audiger's diagrams; it is given a spread tablecloth draped in folds, and some of the pictures show its claw feet peeping out underneath. The plates on the table remain empty, serving as markers for the positions of the dishes at a real-life entertainment (see Figures 24a and b).

The second edition of Henry Howard's *England's*

24a and b
Two tables, one
showing an
arrangement of dishes
for 6 diners, and the
other for 14 or 15
diners, from F.
Massialot, *The Court
and Country Cook*, 1702.

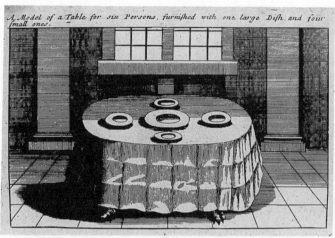

A Model of a Table for six Persons, furnished with one large Dish, and four small ones.

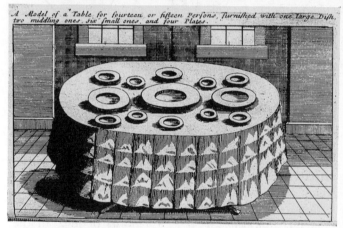

A Model of a Table for fourteen or fifteen Persons, furnished with one large Dish, two middling ones, six small ones, and four Plates.

Newest Way in All Sorts of Cookery, Pastry, and All Pickles that are Fit to be Used, published in 1708, contains the final innovation which was to set the pattern for diagrams of table-settings through the rest of the eighteenth century and beyond. The illustrations for a first and second course appear side by side on a folding-plate. The circles (four large and five smaller, including the one in the middle) are set in positions within an oval representing the table-top.

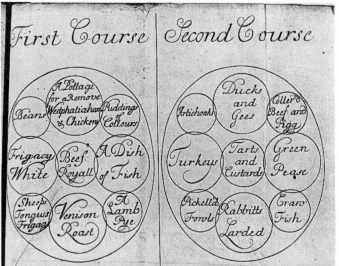

First Course | Second Course

First Course:
A Pottage for a Remove Westphalia ham & Chicken · Puddings of Collours
Beans
Fricacy White · Beef Royall · A Dish of Fish
Sheeps Tongues Frigas · Venison Roast · A Lamb Pye

Second Course:
Ducks and Gees · Coller'd Beef and Pigg
Artichoaks
Turkeys · Tarts and Custards · Green Pease
Pickell'd Fowls · Rabbitts Larded · Cran Fish

25.
Early example of an
English table diagram
with named dishes for
a two-course dinner
from H. Howard,
*England's Newest Way
in all sorts of Cookery*,
third edition, 1710.

Across each one, inscribed in a copperplate hand, is the name of the dish which was to be placed in that position. Thus for the first course the large circle at the foot of the table contains 'venison roast', while 'sheeps tongues fricasey' and 'a lamb pie' are set in the smaller circles to the viewer's left and right respectively. For the second course the large circle in the same position carries 'rabbits larded', the circle to the left 'pickled fowls' and that to the right 'crawfish' (see Figure 25).

This is indeed *England's Newest Way*: there is even the recently adopted usage of the 'remove' (a dish to be succeeded by another). The circle at the head of the first-course table is inscribed: 'A pottage, for a remove Westphalia ham and chickens'. The pottage (very soon to be replaced on the diagrammatic table-settings by one of the new thinner soups) was served out to everyone present, and its large serving-bowl or tureen was then removed. In its place was set the item of meat or fish written in the lower half of the circle. The soup and its 'remove' or replacement marked the first step towards a

different division of the courses which led eventually,
after the coming of Russian service early in the nineteenth
century, to the usual sequence of courses at today's formal
dinners.

In a neat and economical way the table diagrams
succeeded in combining the items on the menu with their
positions on the table, and it is not surprising that this
new visual aid became popular with the writers and
publishers of cookery-books. Many examples of
copperplate engravings on the pattern of those in
England's Newest Way can be found in the more
substantial recipe books published during the rest of the
century. Sometimes the ideal meals they portray were
arranged on a month by month basis, as in Charles
Carter's *The Compleat City and Country Cook* of 1732 (see
Figure 26), and in *The Whole Duty of a Woman*, 1737 (see
Figure 27). Other books contained a smaller number of
illustrations, and the seasonal aspect was limited to a
menu for a dinner in winter and one for a dinner in
summer, as in E. Smith's *The Compleat Housewife* of 1727
(and many later editions) (see Figure 28); though she does
also include diagrams for a two-course supper and for an
'Amlegue'.[11] Martha Bradley's *The British Housewife*, vol. 1,
of *c.* 1760 claims on its title-page to be 'embellished with a
great number of curious copper plates shewing ... the
order of setting out tables for dinners, suppers ... by
which even those who cannot read will be able to
instruct themselves'. And, sure enough, the dishes on
her diagrammatic tables are already filled with
representations of actual food (see Figure 29).

A few cookery writers chose to omit the table diagrams.
Hannah Glasse wrote in the introduction to the famous
folio first edition of *The Art of Cookery*, 1747: 'Nor shall I
take it upon me to direct a Lady how to set out her Table;
for that would be impertinent ... Nor indeed do I think it
would be pretty, to see a Lady's Table set out after the
directions of a Book'. Only after many editions of *The Art*

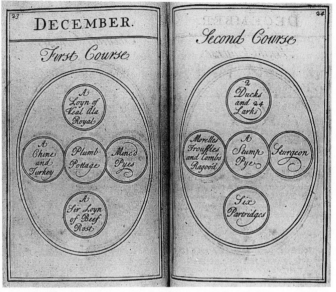

26.
Table-setting for a two-course dinner in December, from C. Carter, *The Compleat City and Country Cook*, 1732.

27.
Table-setting for a two-course dinner in September, from *The Whole Duty of a Woman*, 1737.

of Cookery had appeared was a slight concession made, in the new edition of 1774. It took the form of a very large folding-plate divided into twelve equal sections, each headed by the name of a month and each containing a printed bill of fare for a three-course dinner for that month.

The anonymous author of *The Complete Family Piece: and Country Gentleman and Farmer's Best Guide*, 1736, did not share Hannah Glasse's qualms. The cookery section forms only the first part of the book, but bills of fare were supplied in printed lists, after which some careful advice was offered describing in words the order in which each dish should be set out on the table (see Figure 30). Similarly, the frontispiece of Amelia Chambers' *The Ladies Best Companion* of *c.* 1800 displays the preparations for the table-setting operation. In a well-appointed kitchen a maid is about to serve the family who can be seen through an open door in the background awaiting their meal; while in the foreground there is a small table set out in due order with the dishes on which the food will shortly be carried in (see Figure 31).

When the copperplate table diagrams were adopted, they were not invariably used for 'ideal meals'. Famous cooks, such as Patrick Lamb in *Royal Cookery; or The Complete Court-cook* of 1710 (he had been cook to the English royal families from the days of King Charles II to the reign of Queen Anne, a period of nearly fifty years), and Charles Carter in his large and handsome *The Complete Practical Cook . . . Adorned with Sixty Curious Copper Plates . . .* of 1730, made use of them to record important meals they had cooked for specific occasions. Charles Carter had been cook to the Duke of Argyll and other members of the nobility, and some of his menus claim to be for meals he had served to the king. Patrick Lamb's book has a large folding-plate of a Coronation meal set out in diagram form on a rectangular table (see Figure 18); and other plates showing dinners or suppers for

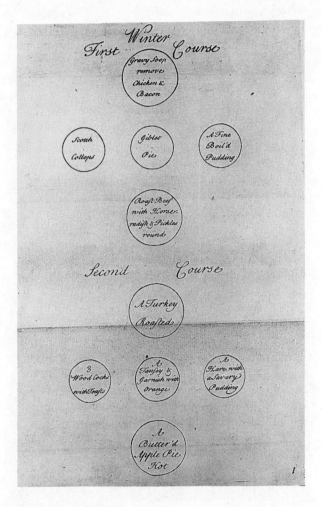

28.
Table-setting for a two-course dinner in winter, from E. Smith, *The Compleat Housewife*, 1727.

29.
Table-setting for a
dinner in May, from
M. Bradley, *The British
Housewife*, vol. 1,
c. 1760.

206   *The Complete* Family-Piece.

Dish of Jellies.
Dish of Fruit.
Quince Pye.

December.

First Course.

Westphalia Ham and Fowls.
Soop with Teal.
Turbet with Shrimps and Oysters.
Marrow Pudding.
Chine of Bacon and Turkey.
Battalio Pye.
Roasted Tongues and Udder, and Hare.

Pullets and Oysters, Sausages, &c.
Minced Pyes.
Cod's Head with Shrimps.

Second Course.

Roasted Pheasants and Partridges.
Bisque of shell Fish.
Tansy.
Dish of roasted Ducks and Teals.
Jole of Sturgeon.
Pear Tart creamed.
Dish of sweet meats.
Dish of Fruit of sorts.

Having given you a Complete Bill of Fare, and Receipts before for dressing almost every Dish mentioned in it, I shall now instruct you how to place your Dishes on the Table ; supposing it then first in the Winter.

At the upper End of your Table place your Dish of Chickens and Bacon, which you must afterwards remove for your Gravy Soop.

Under that Giblet Pye.

On the further Side of which place a fine boiled Pudding.

On the nearer side of the Giblet Pye place Scotch Collops.

And at the Bottom of the Table, place a Dish of Roast Beef with Horse Radish and Pickles round.

Second Course.

At the upper End of the Table a Turkey roasted.

Under that a Tansy garnished with Orange.

On

30.
Bills of fare and verbal instructions on how to position dishes on the table, from *The Complete Family Piece*, 1736.

'Instalments, Balls, Weddings, &c. at Court'. Even the twenty or so more ordinary two-course dinners also illustrated in his book were very probably drawn and engraved on the basis of notes he had kept of particular meals prepared for the royal family and their guests. The recipes for many of the dishes are in the main body of the book, so its purchasers could have attempted to reproduce some of the royal meals shown in the table diagrams for their own guests, if they so wished, and if they had the means to carry out the wish. The diagrams for the great meals for special occasions may also have been studied for pleasure by readers pressing their noses against the window of such a grand entertainment.

The first book to be devoted entirely to menus and table-settings was published in 1760. Its title-page reads: *The Modern Method of Regulating and Forming a Table Explained and Displayed, Containing a Great Variety of Dinners laid out in the Most Elegant Taste, from two Courses of five and five to twenty-one and twenty-one Dishes*. It is an exceptionally large volume, with its pages designed in facing pairs, and it is interesting to find that the copperplate engravings revert to the original convention of the empty plates on the table-top. On the left-hand side of each opening are the empty dishes arranged in due order according to their number and size; on the right-hand side is a printed version of their contents, with each item set out on the page in the corresponding position to its dish on the left. The user would have had no difficulty in matching one with the other (see Figure 32).

The eighteenth-century examples discussed here show that the concept of the 'ideal meal' or sample menu had become very much a part of the cookery literature of the age, whether expressed as a printed bill of fare or as an engraved table diagram. Some people may have followed the suggested menus slavishly, especially those who were trying to rise in the world and to create an impression upon carefully chosen guests. The lady who, in Hannah

FRONTISPIECE.

James Taylor del. et sculp.

Choice Viands, and a skilful Cook, invite
The Puny —— and Capacious Appetite.
Then let **P**oliteness, Join'd to hunger, haste
And learn the Method how to **D**ine in Taste.

31.
Frontispiece showing dishes laid out in order in the kitchen, on which food will shortly be served to the family in the dining-room beyond the hallway, from A. Chambers, *The Ladies Best Companion, c.* 1800.

32.
Table diagram from
The Modern Method of
Regulating and Forming
a Table, 1760.

Glasse's view, should not have been setting out her table 'after the directions of a Book', may nevertheless have consulted a book containing table diagrams to collect fresh ideas about possible combinations of dishes within a course, even if she then re-combined some of the dishes from the book with others of her own choice. The menus for ideal meals leave no historical record of how they were used, or how often the meals were created and for what social occasions. But the frequent appearance of the bills of fare and diagrams of table-settings in eighteenth-century cookery-books suggests that some at least of those meals were served, perhaps many times, in the course of the century.

Notes and References

1. Durham University Library MS Cosin V.iii.11, and British Library MS Cotton Julius D viii, *in* C.B. Hieatt & S. Butler, eds., *Curye on Inglysch* (Early English Text Society, SS 8, 1985), p. 40. Spelling has been modernised here.
2. R. Napier, ed., *A Noble Boke off Cookry (Holkham MS)*, (London, 1882) p. 13.
3. British Library MS Sloane 442. The three menus precede a collection of fifteenth-century cookery recipes collated by Professor C. B. Hieatt with the similar collection in Yale University Library: C. B. Hieatt, ed., *An Ordinance of Pottage (MS Yale Beinecke 163)* (London, 1988), p. 110.
4. T. Austin, ed., *Two Fifteenth-century Cookery-books* (Early English Text Society, OS 91, 1888) p. 67.
5. J. Russell, *Boke of Nurture, in* F. J. Furnivall, ed., *Early English Meals and Manners* (Early English Text Society, OS 32, 1868) pp. 172–3.
6. W. Harrison, *Description of England*, ed. from Holinshed's *Chronicle* 1577 and 1587 by F. J. Furnivall (London, 1877) pp. 148–9 for the new interest in food and cooking among people of the middling sort (with particular emphasis on imported foods). This corresponded with a general rise in the standard of living at all levels of society below the nobility; elsewhere in the same text Harrison discussed this phenomenon in relation to house furnishings.
7. 'A Breviate Touching the Order and Government of a Nobleman's House, 1605', communicated by Sir J. Banks, *Archaeologia* 13 (1800), p. 355.
8. G. Markham, *The English Hus-wife*, 4th ed. (London, 1631) pp. 137–40.

9. J. Murrell, *Murrels Two Books of Cookerie and Carving, the fifth time printed with new Additions* (London, 1638), p. 9.
10. R. May, *The Accomplisht Cook*, 2nd ed. (London, 1665), B8.
11. This must surely be a misreading by the engraver for 'Ambigue', the fashionable one-course supper of the late seventeenth and early eighteenth centuries.

6.

Keeping Up Appearances: The Genteel Art of Dining in Middle-Class Victorian Britain

DENA ATTAR

To start with a riddle: what is the difference between an eel and a hedgehog, or between a croustade of sheep's ears and an ostrich egg? As with the best riddles, there is more than one solution. Moving from the first to the following answers takes us from the obvious to the hidden, from appearances to what lies behind them. *The eel and the hedgehog*

There is over a hundred years' difference in time between the eighteenth-century recipe for a 'hedgehog', a sweet trifle-like pudding or cream stuck all over with almonds for spines, and the nineteenth-century recipe for a stuffed cooked eel mounted to look like, yet fearsomely unlike, itself in its living state. Hannah Glasse included a hedgehog receipt in *The Art of Cookery Made Plain and Easy* (1747); John Middleton had one for a hedgehog cream in *Five hundred new receipts* (1734) and there were quite possibly other published versions. I found the illustrated eel, unattributed, in a twentieth-century anthology of Victorian recipes, and recognised in it an extreme version of many similar portraits of dishes dating from the mid- and late Victorian era. The 'ostrich egg' was another eighteenth-century idea designed to raise a smile – the yolks of hens' eggs cooked in a bladder placed inside several whites, cooked again to produce one huge 'egg'. The croustade, in contrast, was a serious nineteenth-century affair of a dozen or so sheep's ears formally arranged and presented upright within a strictly symmetrical border. There is a serious point in comparing such obviously unlike creations for, after all, they were not meant for everyday family meals but each was designed to be seen and admired by a company of guests. They provide us with evidence, which I would argue can be generalised, of changing tastes and intentions. I would go further and suggest that whoever dreamed up the croustade and eel would hardly be capable of a joke such as the 'ostrich egg'.

33.
Eel with Montpelier butter, from J. H. Walsh, *A Manual of Domestic Economy Suited to Families Spending from £150 to £1500 a Year*, 1879.

34.
Sheep's ears in croustade, from Walsh, *A Manual of Domestic Economy*, 1879.

From a late twentieth-century vantage point, the egg and the hedgehog amuse, and are not particularly distant from dishes in current use. The eel and the sheep's ears are likely to startle us, though, and it is hard to imagine any contemporary cook wishing to present their ingredients in such rigid and complicated forms today. To put the riddle another way: what happened to culinary elegance and wit between the mid-eighteenth and late nineteenth centuries? This is of course a loaded question, and it is framed by a widespread current preference for Georgian over Victorian design, for the style of eighteenth- rather than nineteenth-century cookery-books, architecture, and artefacts of all kinds. Recipes, like buildings, are designed and are the products of specific times and circumstances. There are key features of design in the examples above which show that the visual appearance of food has become significantly more serious and important for the Victorian hostess or host, an observation confirmed by a wealth of other material in cookery and household books. By the late nineteenth century, the 'look' of food has become profoundly non-naturalistic. Even (or perhaps especially) where dishes of raw fruit or plain vegetables are shown, there are many instances of fearful symmetry. Illustrations and recipe designs reveal an exaggerated concern with form and regularity, and a desire to re-present the raw materials involved as a series of discrete objects sometimes related to their natural origins but often having no connection with them.

We are not neutral observers of this 'look'. Victorian design has for decades been associated with fussy architecture and cluttered, sombre interiors. These negative characteristics appear against a perceived background of sexual repression and its inevitable consequence, sexual hypocrisy; of a 'separate spheres' doctrine of womanhood and a suffocating view of femininity as domestic, pure, but above all inferior; of a peculiarly harsh and punitive system of class barriers. The earlier period is credited with virtues such as space, light, outspokenness, appetites celebrated rather than suppressed, generosity rather than ostentatious display. The concepts of Victorian or of Georgian design which are in current use of course represent simplified and selective views of their historical periods, and the fashions and ideas of our own period inevitably shape our reactions to them. I am mindful of these prejudices, and also perhaps more importantly of the need to remember the diversity of Victorian society in Britain. Diet, like so much else, was highly differentiated according to class, sex, age and even state of health to a much greater degree than before or since, and it is particularly striking that all these distinctions between one person's food and another's could exist within a single household. Despite

35.
Croquettes de poulet, Gateaux de saumon, Cotelettes de mouton à la Maintenon, Matelote de poulet, from Walsh, *A Manual of Domestic Economy*, 1879.

these caveats there are still two safe generalisations which can be made about the cuisine of mid-Victorian Britain, and which I aim to show are connected. First, this was a period when the visual appearance of food took precedence over considerations of taste or nutritious value; second, both in the opinions of those who were eating it at the time and in the view of modern scholars, the standard of cooking experienced by a great many people was poor, and declining.

Complaints about bad English food appeared in print well before the period discussed here. Some early nineteenth-century writers – Dr Kitchiner, for one – were vitriolic about the average cook's want of skill, and invoked a lost golden age of superior hospitality when describing their miseries at the dinner table. There is a

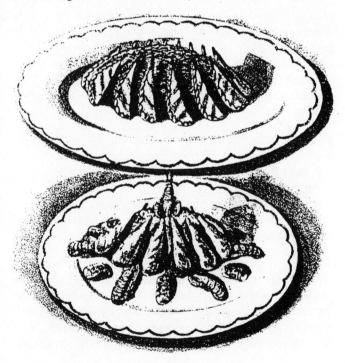

recurring irony in references to the good old days, a period which is no one's present but everyone's past. In this instance, though, food scholars appear to agree with contemporary judgements in seeing a real decline from around the mid-century. Stephen Mennell in *All Manners of Food* (1985) passes a categorical verdict:

> Certainly there is no sense of progress and development in English domestic cookery in the middle and late Victorian period ... With the exception of Acton, it does not seem unfair to describe the food of the nineteenth-century English domestic cookery-books as rather monotonous, and above all lacking in any sense of the enjoyment of food. (p.214).

Mennell's work traces the influence of French cuisine, at times resisted and at other times enthusiastically embraced. He is scathing about the superficial incorporation of elements of French style in food designed for the British mid-Victorian middle class. The example he cites as representative is Cassell's *Dictionary of Cookery* (1875):

> It proclaims 'economy to be the soul of cookery', and the depth of the French influence can be judged from the author's equation of 'entrees' with croquettes and kromeskies made from leftover cold meat, and from his advocacy of flower-shaped pieces of turnip for the adornment of dishes.

Stuck-on decorations and recycled leftovers were not random features of recipe design but were integral to this particular system of food usage. We have to look at the factors which determine different cuisines – the food supply itself, the labour resource, and the influence of fashion – for an explanation. The questions to answer are, what is there to cook? Who is doing the cooking and what are they trying to do?

The croquette, not-so-distant ancestor of the school dinner spam fritter, was surely an urban invention. It can be plausibly located within an aspiring middle-class household which was affluent enough to afford large joints, but could not afford to simply finish up the cold meat. What was wanted was a genteel-looking dish, not too messy, which could be made to look dainty – a favourite mid-Victorian adjective – but employed the essential virtue of thrift. How it tasted was a secondary consideration. It would not have been ladylike for the mistress of the house to take too much of an interest in how her food tasted anyway. Whether she or her servant cooked, skilfully or not, they were dealing with essentially unfamiliar dishes.

A closer look at the croquette

Mennell described English cookery in this period as 'decapitated' – the professional cooks in Britain having no national leadership of their own, but deferring absolutely to the French. It is perhaps even more true to describe the cooking in many British homes as having lost its roots. The Roast remained, of course, for every household which could afford it, an important symbol of wealth, status and national character even if it distorted the food budget for the rest of the week. The pudding in all its varieties hung on too, eventually dislodged from first to last place in the order of the meal. For the rest, the overall pattern seemed to be of unfamiliar dishes cooked by one class for another, although neither group had much idea of how the food should taste, nor were they encouraged to care.

The pattern of dining on joints, or other large and expensive items, followed by a series of meals based on the leftovers seemed ideally suited to households providing a number of meals at different times to people who could not share the same food. Even if the family was small, servants would not eat with their employers, and children would be served their food separately at least for the last meal of the day. It was accepted that food provided for servants would be cheaper and simpler, and although some domestic manuals warned against expecting servants to accept scraps from the family's plates for their own use, their main meals would very often consist of rehashes and *réchauffés*. Children were thought to need the plainest food with the emphasis on bread, preferably stale, and pudding rather than meat. (Some medical advisers warned middle-class mothers that raw fruit and lightly cooked vegetables were positively harmful to children.) 'Sick cookery', as it was known, featured as a separate section in almost every cookery-book and household or medical manual and, as most illnesses were nursed at home, an additional separate diet would often be required for the resident invalid.

There is a portrait of a typical hierarchical subdivision of the joint plus leftovers in Alexis Soyer's *The Modern Housewife* (1849). Soyer's receipts for the housewife were given alongside a sketchy account of a shopkeeper's rise to greater prosperity, which enabled his family to enlarge the scope of their housekeeping and eat ever more elaborate meals. Mr and Mrs B were eventually able to dine on 'one soup or fish (generally alternate) – one remove, either joint or poultry – one entree – two vegetables – pudding or tart – a little dessert'. The fictional Mrs B explained that this basic menu was not as extravagant as it appeared:

This may seem a great deal for two persons; but when you remember that we almost invariably have one or two to dine with us, and the remains are required for the breakfast, lunch, nursery and servants' dinners, you will perceive that the dinner is the principal expense of the establishment, by which means you are enabled to display more liberality to your guests, and live in greater comfort without waste.

Diners à la Russe. **701**

36.
Table plan for Diners à
la Russe, from Walsh,
*A Manual of Domestic
Economy,* 1879.

costs more than the above sum, but as the remains will feed the household for a week, the difference from the usual whole weekly expenditure will not be more than £5 or £6, unless every delicacy of the season is considered indispensable. At all events, it is a fact, that many people celebrated for the pleasantness of their dinner parties, confine themselves to the above sum.

2662. Diners à la Russe.

The annexed plan on the scale of half an inch to one foot shows a table set out à la Russe for a party of eighteen, one-half of it being further illustrated in colours opposite page 702.

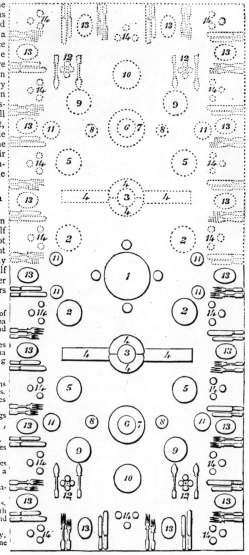

1. — Central vase of flowers with four china shells grouped round it.
2.... 2, — Glass dishes supported by china figures containing fruits, &c.
3, 3,—Candelabra.
4.... 4,—Glass troughs containing cut flowers.
5.... 5, — China dishes containing fruit.
6, 6,—Glass water jugs on
7. 7,—Velvet stands.
8.... 8,—Glass goblets.
9.... 9, — China dishes containing fruit.
10.... 10,—China vases each containing a plant.
11.... 11, — Water caraffes.
12.... 12,—Small cruets.
13.... 13—Napkins with bread and knives and forks arranged.
14.... 14, — Sherry, claret, and champagne glasses.

37.
Diner à la Russe: half-
table for eighteen,
from Walsh, *A manual
of Domestic Economy,*
1879.

DINER A LA RUSSE—HALF TABLE FOR EIGHTEEN.   p. 702.

The emphasis here is on economical display, which
became the basis of the cuisine in a growing number of
households in the decades after Soyer's advice was
published, as the middle classes continued to rise and to
include in their ranks more people who had reason to feel
insecure about their status and standard of living. Soyer
took an interest in the food of the poor, as did Charles
Francatelli, who was Queen Victoria's cook but also
published *A Plain Cookery Book for the Working Classes*
(1852). Both men advised the poorest sections of society
on economical soups and other cheap dishes using
language which is never to be found in their other works.
Francatelli recommended one of his dishes to his readers
as a 'savoury mess'. I have found no instance of these or
similar words applied to recipes for the middle class. Soyer
and Francatelli made frequent references to nutritional

qualities and taste in their recipes for the poor. We take for granted the absence of such references in cookery-books for the middle class, although the cost is often mentioned and the appearance of a dish is sometimes its only *raison d'être*.

Elaborately decorated dishes have a long history, from mediaeval 'subtleties' to seventeenth-century banqueting conceits, to *pièces montées* in the nineteenth century. The stress on ornamentation was not itself new in this period; the important change was its extension to a widening audience. Conceits and subtleties were designed as the centrepieces for aristocratic tables. Carême, the most lauded of the professional cooks at the beginning of the nineteenth century, liked to decorate his dishes very much in the aristocratic style with skewers bearing coats of arms or other emblems. Soyer's biographer, Helen Morris, maintained that Soyer never sacrificed the palate to the eye, but there is no doubt that he saw the visual appearance of a dish as highly important, even if it could sometimes be treated as a joke. He claimed in *The Gastronomic Regenerator* (1845) that it was against his principles 'to have any unnecessary ornamental work in a dinner', but this – in an introduction to ornamental croustades of bread for removes – merely tells us something of what Soyer considered necessary. He frequently gave instructions for the precise shape and size to which vegetables should be trimmed, and a good number of his recipes were simply step-by-step compilations of pre-cooked ingredients, assembled with an eye to colour and shape. The croquette, like the many bombes, moulds and jellies which became popular in the late nineteenth century (Francatelli used aspic in scores of his recipes), was only a down-market version of the expensive creations produced for the tables of wealthier employers, and it was the perfect choice for those who had to eat up their own leftovers but were too genteel to want 'savoury messes'.

Pot plants on the Between the first and last years of Victoria's reign the rules
table about how a genteel dining table should look were utterly
changed. At the beginning of the period service was still *à
la française*, with a large number of dishes placed on the
table at once in a sequence of two main courses preceded
by soup and followed by dessert. This system had held in
Britain for a long time, and although originally diners
would have helped themselves and each other it
eventually required a large number of servants in the most
formal households, sometimes one behind each chair, to
ensure that dishes were handed round. It was gradually
superseded by dinners *à la Russe*, with more courses each
containing fewer dishes. The two main effects of this
changeover both suited the aspiring middle classes and
made entertaining possible on a tighter budget. Fewer
servants were needed – it was even possible to manage
with a single servant fetching and clearing dishes. It was
also no longer necessary to cover the table with impressive
numbers and types of plates of food. The hostess could
provide less, and guests would have less choice, but
instead the table itself could be decorated.

Eighteenth-century cookery-books often included,
either as a frontispiece or later in the book, one or more
plans of table-settings for a fixed number of persons. The
number of dishes on offer would generally increase with
the number of guests, and each dish had its proper
position on the table. The table plan was at once a guide
for arranging the dishes symmetrically and effecting a
balanced distribution of pies, roasts, corner-dishes and so
forth – necessary with perhaps fifteen or twenty different
items – and a menu. Pictures and plans in mid-Victorian
books also showed symmetrical arrangements, but
frequently without the food. Instead there was a profusion
of objects, some for use and others for show. The
centrepiece was no longer something to be eaten, the
word 'centrepiece' having changed its meaning to refer to
a receptacle of glass, china or metal holding flowers,

candles or both. Flower arranging for the table became a subject in its own right, as did the folding of table napkins, and books were written on both these branches of entertaining. In one domestic manual of 1879 (J. H. Walsh, *A manual of domestic economy*) readers were even advised that the difference between a modest and a lavish outlay when giving a dinner depended on the flowers selected for the decorations.

Walsh's manual included an engraved plan, with the aid of which 'the inexperienced housekeeper may venture to adopt the dîner à la Russe'. Almost everything shown in the plan could be hired, the manual advised, and there were ways of constructing cheap centrepieces, using drooping ferns to hide the shape of the improvised structure which saved the cost of an expensive ornament. Even plants could be hired, if a household could not supply its own plants and flowers. From the central vase of flowers with its surrounding group of china shells down to the velvet stands on which the water jugs were placed, the focus of attention was not on food but on things, not surprisingly in an era when more people were owning more things, and factory manufacture and the Empire between them ensured the supply of ever more objects to own. A pastrycook could supply the dinner itself, which was given only a passing mention compared with the attention paid to the table arrangements. There is one towering confection on the dinner table illustrated in the manual, accompanied by a few other edible items displayed on pedestalled dishes with doilies, but they are almost hidden by the carafes and candelabra, ferns, aspidistra and statuary which hit the eye first.

In these circumstances it hardly needed saying that the potatoes ought all to be peeled to a uniform size and arranged in a pyramid, and it made sense for cooks to boil cabbages, whole, for a good half hour in gallons of water, then drain them and press them and serve them in sauce so that at least they would look neat. The food, when it arrived, would have to compete with the ornamental display the table presented even before the start of a meal. It was impossible to serve messy looking food in such surroundings: hence the need for so many moulds and frills, médaillons, zéphires and stamped-out shapes. Even in the nursery there was one pudding known simply as 'shape'.

A history of the Cookery-books and domestic manuals can be unreliable
doily witnesses to the history of food presentation, since we cannot be sure how much notice was taken of them, or the extent to which they reflect the custom of the day. The history of the doily is a tale which in its own way confirms the theme of this chapter, that as people further down the social scale began to entertain, the appearance of each dish and of the dinner table became more important to more people, although how the food tasted mattered less.

Mr Doily, or Doyley, was a seventeenth-century linen draper who kept a shop in the Strand, 'a little West of Catherine Street' (Pegge, quoted in the OED). He gave his name to a woollen fabric first used for summer clothing, which the *Spectator* in 1712 described as 'at once cheap and genteel'. In time the word came to mean an ornamental napkin, originally called a doily-napkin, which was used at dessert. Jonathan Swift wrote in 1711, 'After dinner we had coarse Doiley-napkins. fringed at each end, upon the table to drink with.' In 1855 Harriet Martineau put in her autobiography, 'I had been picking at the fringe of my doily', but although still fringed the doily by that date was no longer coarse. It was also about to acquire an even more genteel name: *Enquire within upon fancy needlework* (1868) included patterns for two D'Oyleys, one netted and one bejewelled.

The function of the doily changed gradually until it became entirely ornamental rather than useful, used for placing underneath articles of food rather than as an ordinary napkin. It was usually round rather than square, always fringed or edged with a patterned border and sometimes lacy throughout. Manuals did not illustrate or recommend the use of a doily only for greasy food, where it might have a function. Green salad, in a complex jellied form, is shown sitting on a doily in one picture, the doily providing the required ornamental edging all around the food. You can spot doilies in many photographs and drawings in late nineteenth- and early twentieth-century books, beneath items as diverse as chicken creams and steaks of cod. By the twentieth century, paper versions were available for hygienic reasons and to save washing, and can still be bought for the ritual occasions which require them now.

The doily had exactly the right characteristics, being at once cheap and genteel. It kept up appearances without straining the resources of the hostess. The authors of cookery and domestic manuals showed a keen awareness of the need for ideas of this kind, none more so than Mrs Alfred Praga, author of *Dinners of the day*, *Starting housekeeping*, and of the marvellously named *Appearances: how to keep them up on a limited income* (1899).

Gender and gentility

Keeping up appearances was a serious business, but I do not mean to suggest that women of all classes were grimly setting out to impress one another with their material wealth and genteel taste without reflecting on what they were doing. In my grandmother's time fish had to be bought whole and first served up grandly, then made to last for days to the dismay of at least some of her household. The fact that she used the expression "Lace curtains and kippers", suggests she was well aware of the genteel charades women put on for public consumption to conceal frugality within the household. In the course of writing this article I was told of other similar (and often ruder) expressions, and of the practice in some households of sharpening the carving knife publicly on the front step before going inside to dine on the equivalent of the kippers – there may have been nothing to carve, but the fictional roast saved face. The pretence was important even if no one was in the least taken in. This was also the point of a scene in one Victorian novel – Mrs Gaskell's elderly heroine in *Cranford* put on a genteel charade at her tea-party, pretending to be surprised by the arrival of the cakes which everyone present knew she had baked herself earlier in the day. Meals are a rich source of social comment in Mrs Gaskell's novels: in *Wives and Daughters* the doctor's new wife will not allow him cheese because of its lack of gentility, so that eating cheese becomes a symbolic act of rebellion for father and daughter when the stepmother is away.

The concept of gentility had a lot to do with gender. In a society where wealth and power were so unequally distributed, it was necessary for the sex and the classes which had much the greatest share of both to maintain a belief in a natural basis for this inequality. Women were thus deemed to have desires, needs and capacities absolutely different from men of their class, and working-class men and women were likewise supposedly incapable of appreciating, even of desiring, the lifestyle of their social superiors. Genteel taste was in effect an expression of these differences. Logically then ladies would be expected to prefer food and drink which shared the essential qualities ascribed to their own natures, and would avoid anything considered too masculine or coarse.

Gender divisions extended right through from the seasoning of a salad to the carving of a fowl. Soyer recommended leaving garlic out of a salad if ladies were to be present at a meal, because they would dislike its strong taste. Chapters on carving in etiquette manuals advised that the wing of a bird was the portion which should be allocated to a lady. The roast represented uncompromisingly masculine taste, but the gentility displayed at the dinner table was predominantly feminine in style, its frills and fussiness an echo of contemporary fashions in dress and interior decoration, which signified a constrained femininity. Gentlemen could have hearty appetites and so could both men and women of the working-class, but dainty morsels were considered to be more fitting for a lady.

38.
Trifle, ices and jellies around, from Walsh, *A Manual of Domestic Economy*, 1879.

The factors which made the appearance of food, and especially a particular kind of appearance, so much more important than its qualities of taste or nutritional worth also served to undermine cookery as a skill. Most cooks were women, but the small minority of male cooks were better paid and more respected. Women cooks often had to prepare food which was either not designed for their own class or for which they were not supposed to have much appetite, and there was a definite ambivalence about ladies working in kitchens since cooking was an activity appropriate to their sex but not their class. The much-lamented awfulness of English food was at least in part a product of English gentility.

There are still more questions, and other ways of answering the riddle. The profoundly unnatural 'look' of Victorian food which put so much distance between the genteel diner and the coarse productions of nature could doubtless be analysed with reference to the psychology of the times, and a contemporary inability to deal honestly with bodily appetites. Although the rules are less rigid and the boundaries have become blurred, in some ways the framework inherited from a century ago remains with us. It would not be hard to find examples today of food recreated in forms which the Victorians would have called dainty, at the expense of other culinary considerations. It could even be argued that whenever anyone fries mashed potato coated and shaped into a croquette, they are paying unwitting tribute to the Victorian art of genteel dining.

Notes and References

Francatelli, Charles, *A plain cookery book for the working classes*, Routledge, Warne and Routledge, (London, 1852; reprinted 1977, Scolar Press, London).

Glasse, Hannah, *The art of cookery, made plain and easy*, printed for the author (London, 1747).

Mennell, Stephen, *All manners of food*, Basil Blackwell (Oxford, 1985).

Middleton, John, *Five hundred new receipts*, Thomas Astley (London, 1734).

Morris, Helen, *Portrait of a chef*, Oxford University Press (Oxford, 1938, reprinted 1980).

Oxford English Dictionary, Oxford University Press, (Oxford, 1971).

Philp, Robert Kemp, *Enquire within upon everything, to which is added Enquire within upon fancy needlework*, Houlston & Sons (London, 1868).

Soyer, Alexis, *The gastronomic regenerator* (London, 1845).

Soyer, Alexis, *The modern housewife*, (London, 1849).

Walsh, John Henry, *A manual of domestic economy*, George Routledge and Sons, (London 1879).

Acknowledgments to A. and R. Bradley, G. Chester and E. Thynne for useful comments on the ideas in this chapter.

7.

Illusion and Illustration in English Cookery-books since the 1940s

LYNETTE HUNTER

The illustration of cookery-books in England since the 1940s has moved inexorably toward a consciousness of the cultural implications or meanings of design, arrangements, food choice and food display. This awareness is a result of a web of technological change in the development of book illustration, as well as social and cultural change in the purpose of the cookery-book, changes in food supply and distribution, and possibly most of all changes in the way we look at 'pictures', at representations of objects.

It was not standard for cookery-books to be illustrated before the 1950s, but there are two or three strands defining those that were: the first comprised the heavily illustrated books deriving from magazines, such as *Mrs Beeton's Household Management* which from the beginning of the century had used colour plates for representing the arrangement and display of dishes and black and white drawings or photographs to illustrate techniques and utensils. The second, related, strand of books was that written by media personalities: journalists or well-known teachers, such as Elizabeth Craig; these books tended again to use photographic illustration, but more judiciously than the magazines and some moved toward decorative drawing in the 1930s and 1940s. The third strand of illustrated cookery-book was rather more specialised, often focusing on the pictures rather than the writing, and was clearly influenced by the Arts and Crafts movement and the experiments with woodcuts and line drawings, particularly by Eric Gill and David Jones.

By the 1940s, it was becoming widely recognised that naïve, 'naturalistic' photographic representation of arrangements, techniques and utensils, was in effect misleading. Book illustrators were becoming more conscious of the constructed factors in their pictures, and the concept of 'enhancing' an illustration to highlight the message it was supposed to be getting across was becoming more important. Indeed it can be argued that the use of techniques deriving from the private press movement were also a response to this recognition of the limitations of photographic representation.

Popular cookery-books of the 1950s and 1960s: the publishing houses The year 1950 saw the publication of Elizabeth David's *A Book of Mediterranean Food*,[1] and in 1951 came the first publication of *Good Housekeeping's Picture Cookery*.[2] The latter revived the failing blockbuster tradition with intelligent use of illustration pioneered by the reproduction techniques of magazine publication. The former gave readers a well-written cookery-book, conceived as a whole, which addressed itself to techniques and foodstuffs beyond the traditional English fare, and a book which was 'decorated' by John Minton. Although writers like Dora Seton whose books follow the earlier Craig tradition did succeed in the 1950s, *Good Housekeeping* and Elizabeth David in many ways defined the parameters for illustrated cookery-books emerging in the 1960s and 1970s. We should not forget that a large number of highly popular writers like Philip Harben (*Woman's Realm*), Sheila Hutchins (*Daily Express*) or Fanny and Johnny Craddock (*Daily Telegraph*) produced books which were not illustrated at all. Individual writers who were able to influence the illustration of their books, were and are in a privileged position. For the majority of readers the illustrated cookery-book is synonymous with the design-led productions of the large publishing houses.

To begin with *Good Housekeeping*: In the early days of the *Good Housekeeping Cookery Book* (1925)³ edited by Florence Jack in the 1920s and 1930s, there were no illustrations. Instructions for icing a child's birthday cake say 'Decorate according to fancy' (p.169). But during the 1940s line-drawings of simple utensils or techniques were introduced, along with black and white photographs of more difficult procedures such as gutting a rabbit or icing a cake. By 1950 the editors of *Good Housekeeping's Picture Cookery* could claim that they had produced 'pictorial cookery booklets' for several years, and that there was 'world-wide demand' for their 'unique publication' (p.6). They went on to say that the purpose of the cookery-book was that 'pictures tell the story better than words'; moreoever, here was

> a book for the many people who gain confidence and knowledge only after they have seen exactly how to carry out a process, and what the finished product should really look like. (p. 6)

Published by the National Magazine Company, *Picture Cookery* is a large format book led from the start by the use of illustrations. The stuck-down endpapers are in colour, and present a step-by-step method of cooking – elsewhere in the book all step-by-step cookery is in black and white. Each section is headed by a two-sided coloured plate relating to the, contents. The fish section begins with a picture of fish, neatly laid out in a pyrex dish, with parsley strategically placed over each eye. The verso shows oysters spilling artistically from a wicker basket, against a tidy arrangement of oysters laid out on a plate. Some of these section headers are rather artificial still-life attempts, but the designer or illustrator is often happy simply to suggest this as a background and show a naturalistic close-up within it. Many black and white photographs are devoted to techniques, ingredients, food preparation, cooking devices, decoration and serving suggestions. A number of colour plates are also used strategically to indicate food status: the table settings always have good china and 'real' silver. The photographic black and white illustrations also borrow from the experience of the line-drawing/ woodcut/engraving tradition which substitutes 'suggestive' groupings of ingredients for an uninteresting depiction of stew, or decorative serving dishes to cheer up the presentation of bland-looking soups.

What the book achieves is a sense of food as entertaining and food preparation as an enjoyable, semi-artistic leisure pursuit rather than domestic drudgery. The step-by-step illustrations are busy, set in what appear to be actual backgrounds rather than the sterile environments of earlier illustrated books which felt like advanced school texts. Yet there is no mess, no untidiness, and the food conforms to an idealised version of its presentation. An inquiring eye notes the lacquered shininess of a roast, the too-bright-to-be-cooked vegetables in the Scotch broth, the more subtle message of exquisitely decorated *petits fours* on an ordinary wire rack telling you that you too can carry out this delicate task. The sophistication of approach, despite its illusions, conveys more about the delight in the taste and smell of food than the naïve representations of many earlier photographs. Where the tradition goes off the rails is over the subsequent twenty years of increasingly artificial food presentation in cookery-books which renders the food itself merely an element in design. This feeds back into cookery itself with trends in the 1970s which take over certain foodstuffs and specific food presentations simply for their design elements, for example the use in nouvelle cuisine of Japanese foods and presentations.

Finding the balance between representation and actual eating habits is immensely difficult to achieve, and there is an element of fun in the emerging techniques which I personally prefer to the self-consciously serious attitude of some food illustration. In 1950 also came the publication of *The Gourmet* cook-book published by *Gourmet Magazine* in New York. The full-colour photograph frontispiece of a crystal, silver and china dinner-table setting immediately stakes out its wealthy audience. The other photographs included in the text return to the earlier use of coloured plates for presentation, which concentrate on table settings or demonstrations of perfectly prepared dishes, such as the lurid bright candy pink of glazed tongue (opp. p. 346). Techniques, utensils and foodstuffs are kept to high-quality line-drawings. But whereas *Good Housekeeping*'s message is addressed to a housewife, assuring her that with a little extra guidance she too can easily achieve all this, *Gourmet*'s message is 'serious', more status-conscious, indicating that you may possibly be able to achieve 'all this' if you copy it exactly. And, further, that if you manage to achieve it you have a passport into the circle of the wealthy or fashionable which already enjoys it. Food and its context can convey power: the appearance of the end product counts for a lot more than the process. Yet the 1958 edition of Elizabeth Ayrton's *Good Simple Cookery*[4] also with step-by-step black and white photographs and colour plates for presentation, moves at times unproductively in the opposite direction in its attempts to be honest. Interesting experiments with Mondrian-type backgrounds jostle with naturalistic presentations of green peppers and tomatoes on cooked kebabs which look as they should, wrinkled and squashed – quite unappetising without the familiar smell.

During the 1960s much of this highly illustrated picture cookery began to become standardised. The great blockbusters of *Good Housekeeping* and their like remained immensely popular, and appear to have been designed in-house by the relevant magazine company, adapting new reproduction technologies as they came along. In the early 1960s the media personalities also emerge, some like

Marguerite Patten under the umbrella of a publisher. In this case, the cookery-book was very much the product of Paul Hamlyn's publishing house and its well-known design team, as well as that of the writer. *A to Z Cookery in Colour* (1963)[5] credits the cover photo but gives no acknowledgement for design or pictures; and the photographs are nearly all of food presentations. However, Patten's *Step-by-Step Cookery* (1963)[6] also with Hamlyn, gives pictures of techniques and presentations with several full-page still-life illustrations (for example see the plate, opposite p. III), and provides many acknowledgements for pictures. In a rather different genre, Nancy Spain's *The Colour Cookery Book* (1963)[7] was published by the packaging firm World Distributors, and professionally designed by 'Vaughan Publishing Services Ltd. London'. In these cases the books, in contrast to those by earlier individual writers such as Elizabeth Craig, depend upon a design team as much as *Good Housekeeping* does.

Popular cookery-books of the 1950s and 1960s: writers and illustrators
A parallel tradition focusing on line-drawings burgeoned throughout the 1950s and 1960s, and emerged predominantly in books by individual writers. Elizabeth David's already mentioned *Mediterranean Food* is an indicative landmark not only for the quality and extent of the writing but also for the integration of illustration and text. Significantly, John Minton's drawings 'decorate' the work rather than illustrate it. David apparently had little say in what Minton produced,[8] yet the drawings pick up on the escapist theme subliminally present in any cookery-book about foreign food. The frontispiece shows two people relaxing in a Mediterranean setting, and the decorated title-page provides detail of the background. There are stylised, rather fantasised pictures of food served on rustic kitchen tables, and there is a focus on the depiction of ingredients rather than kitchen technology.

French Country Cooking which was published the

following year (1951)[9] is also 'decorated' by John Minton. But here there is much more attention to detail and an almost narrative presentation of the interlocking of countryside, cooking and serving. Rather than the distance of the earlier eye, we find here an invitation to involvement into the life around the food – for example the frontispiece is of a woman working in a provincial kitchen. Elizabeth David has commented that she had by this time made friends with Minton, and encouraged 'a theme which recurred in all, or nearly all, of my subsequent books. I wanted the illustrations to convey information, not just atmosphere'. There were to be no gratuitous jolly peasants or dangling vines.

Both these early books were written during the period of rationing after the Second World War. Each provides sensible advice on larders, the use of tinned food, possible places to buy imported foreign produce. The writing itself offers both clear instruction and an invitation to escape, by way of food, from the grey tighten-your-belt mentality of the post-war years. The illusion in the illustrations is an open declaration of intent as to the purpose of cooking and enjoying this food, and one that is not aimed at efficiency, status, or drudgery-is-fun, but at developing a more conscious awareness of the possibilities in the context of the food supply available at the time. This rather serious intent is somewhat diverted by the decoration, but also lightened and made more acceptable. A contrast may be found in the 'drawings by Renato Guttuso' in *Italian Food* (1954)[10] which are bold, actual, stark and curiously formal. On the whole they emphasise pure ingredients (egg and lemon), straightforward cooking (frying pan), and basic eating (wine and bread): food at its most simple and immediate. There is little in terms of decorative cultural background, and the drawings complement the tone of the text which claims to present these foods as commonly accessible, opening awareness of taste to anyone.

What is significant about all the illustrations in these early David books is their concentration on context rather than naturalistic presentation. The move is echoed in David Gentleman's illustrations for *Plats du Jour* by Patience Grey and Primrose Boyd (1957)[11] and followed by many writers with their publishers during the next decade. *The Alice B. Toklas Cook Book*[12] with illustrations by Sir Francis Rose is just one instance of a symbiotic relationship between drawing and text. The writing is humorous in its own way, and is matched by the jokes of the artist in pictures such as 'Dishes for Artists', 'Murder in the Kitchen', a framed 'Still-Life' and the vegetable people of the later pages. The artist recognises that the focus of the collection lies in the personality of Toklas as he depicts a woman calmly eating a pear in the frontispiece.

Just as in the earlier work of Elizabeth Craig, many writers transferred over into the use of decorative line-drawings rather than photographs. One long-running example of the shift is Dora Seton's *Essentials of Modern Cookery*,[13] first published in 1945 with no pictures, and with overt claims to scientific efficiency in the 'FHCI, Dipd Econ (Lond)...' of the title page. The 1956 edition[14] adds photographs for techniques such as filleting or icing, and identification of odd vegetables. In 1957 the book is renamed *Cookery with the Professional Touch*, as the perception of its audience shifts from post-school text readers to people with a more status-conscious interest in catering and restaurants: recipes for hors d'oeuvres are included for the first time. But by 1965, still with the same publisher of 1945 (Evans Brothers), the book has been personalised into *Dora Seton's Cookery Book with Illustrations by Owen J. Thorpe*. 'FHCI . . . etc' has disappeared, as have all the photographs, which have been replaced by decorative line-drawings that set an atmosphere. As if the Elizabeth David approach has been passed through a magazine filter, the full-colour photographic cover depicts 'natural' ingredients on a wooden table, backed by glass jars of seasonings and herbs. Many other books emerge in this hybrid genre, some such as Bee Nilson's *The Career Woman's Cookbook* (1966)[15] indicating far greater interdependence with the line-drawings of ingredients, here by Yvonne Skargon, despite the glossy 'message' cover with tomato/onion/green pepper alongside bracelet and lipstick.

Yvonne Skargon went on to illustrate many of Jane Grigson's books. Grigson's work makes for a useful study since it was published both in book form and in magazine articles for *The Observer* over many years. The different modes of publication have called forward quite different considerations in illustration. Grigson stated that her books did not require illustration in the sense of decoration,[16] but that there is a need for drawings for the purposes of identification, particularly botanical identification. This writer also had a special interest in book design[17] and recognised the contribution that illustration can make to a 'nice-looking, elegant book'. Just as important is the typography and the design of the page, which can present the writing without pretention. Grigson's quest for the simple and unpretentious is noted in her choice of Ben Nicolson as the artist who would have most clearly satisfied her desire for the 'single line ∴.. that perfectly describes, entirely suggests [the] mass and volume' of the foodstuffs she would want to depict.

Trends in the 1970s: writers and illustrators

A similar concern with identification can be found in the books by Alan Davidson. His geographically organised books on seafood provide detailed black and white drawings of the species and varieties particular to the location. He notes that photographs are actually quite difficult for this work since the depiction of a living fish may be misleading because, for example, colour often changes when the fish dies yet photographs of dead fish tend to look like just that: pictures of corpses.[18] In contrast, the black and white line-illustration can achieve accuracy and appeal. *North Atlantic Seafood*[19] uses illustrations by a variety of artists, many from the late nineteenth and the early twentieth centuries. While considerable effort has gone into harmonising the look of each two-page spread, the variety brings an interest and fresh attention to each biological presentation which might otherwise have become repetitive and tedious to follow. The book also uses black and white prints and depictions of local artefacts to convey an historical point, and the writer cites for example the barge at Leningrad (p. 6), which presents a context that would otherwise have made necessary a lot of writing, and that also makes the reader think about the topic in a rather different way.

Unusually, Davidson had a total grasp of the procedures for illustrating this and his other seafood books,[20] but in his recent *Fasting and Feasting* (1988)[21] the publishers intervened quite extensively. There, the art director of the publishing house had the idea of using pastel reproductions of old masters and was primarily concerned with design. But Davidson says that the artist, Susan Alcantarilla, was in much closer contact with him and read all the articles. The result is again a thought-provoking book where the illustrations, such as that of the famous *Folies Bergère* café transformed into a *charcuterie* counter (pp. 154–5), are in the writer's words 'disconcerting but amiable'. In the view of some critics, more disconcerting than amiable. However, the technique does provide an intelligent use of the ubiquitous presence of the full-page colour plate, which Davidson himself says is often overdone; and in de-mythologising the Old Masters, the illustrations also help to de-mythologise the current high-priest status of food writers.

Neither did Jane Grigson generally find colour plates of paintings particularly helpful to her work. This may be because much of her work focused on cooking in England, and she noted that English artists have anyway consistently avoided depicting foodstuffs for their own sake. There are no great portrayals by, say, Reynolds or Stubbs to compare with the history of depicting food in other European traditions. It may be also that the publishers who have included this kind of illustration in Grigson's work – Macmillan in *English Food,* Cape in *Exotic Fruit and Vegetables* –have not been sensitive to the requirements of the text or of the design. Certainly Grigson recognised that the case for food illustration in magazines is quite different. Her *Observer* magazine articles were always accompanied by colour photographs from the late 1960s to the present, and appear to have suffered only minimally from the excesses of 'designer' food illustration which were hovering during this period. In interview, Grigson recounted the story of one of her earlier photographic illustrators sitting down and eating the meal as soon as he had photographed it, as an example of the absence of fakery, of delusory intervention, in these magazine illustrations. Yet she also criticised the increasingly important role of the 'food stylist' who has come to assume responsibility for the appearance of the food photograph, without necessarily recognising that the food should take precedence over the design. The story is told of an occasion when her daughter, the food writer Sophie Grigson, was asked to put red pepper into a recipe simply because the stylist wanted to make the dish more beautiful.

The focus of the magazine tradition on design has not often been so pleasingly handled as in the case of Jane Grigson's articles. As with the in-house publications of the early 1960s referred to earlier, the influence of a design team has been a decidedly mixed blessing. It led in the 1970s to cookery comics, cookery coffee-table books, and more extensively into the conglomerate serial publications by, for example, *Time-Life* or newspaper magazines. It feeds into the re-emergence of 'great chef'

Trends in the 1970s: publishers and designers

books over the last ten to fifteen years. Last, and of enormous influence, it becomes rooted in developments surrounding the presentation of food in advertising.

The initial focus on design in food illustration derived immediately from the recognition that 'naturalistic' photography was just not working. Rather than turn to line-drawing, many design teams tackled the problems of presentation and illusion in use of the photographic illustration, hunting out the arrangements, angles of vision, details of colour, size, background, that conformed to the current expectations of the public perception of food. Work by designers for the press was necessarily concerned with the immediate impact of the photograph; the text in an advertisement or a glossy magazine may often be of little importance. If the picture has to carry the burden of telling the story then the food photographer displaces the role of the writer; the 'author' becomes the design team – and nowhere more so than in publishing house productions.

A typical design team may consist of the home economist who specialises in food presentation, the food stylist, the food photographer and the designer who oversees the entire process and consults with each part of the group. The home economist is responsible for buying the fresh ingredients, of the right shape and size and colour, and for cooking the food correctly for the camera: for example the oranges on a plate may have to be exactly round, the picture of a 3lb joint of lamb for a recipe will probably need to be of a 5lb joint because of shrinkage in cooking, and the home economist will need to know exactly when to stop the cooking time so the dish looks at its best – never mind about taste. The stylist is concerned with the look of the food, supplies props, ensures that a mushy stew appears colourful, devises ways of making a stuffed pepper (with most of the ingredients inside it) generate interest, or a lettuce leaf seem as fresh as it did at five o'clock in the morning market. The photographer may arrange the food, set the lighting and background, and will of course be concerned with angle, focus, scope and so on, of the final picture.

Given that the illustration must be an illusion in the sense that it must be constructed to conform to the viewer's perceptions of what food should look like, it appears to be at the stylist's place in the procedure that the rather more tricky elements emerge. During the 1960s and 1970s many deceptions were invented to help the design along: putting stones in the bottom of a bowl of soup to raise the level of liquid,[22] blowing cigarette smoke through a straw to simulate steam,[23] covering green paper with glycerine to fake lettuce,[24] cooking the white of an egg first and cutting a round hole in it for the raw yolk to present the perfect fried egg,[25] actually painting the food the 'right' colour – the list is endless. These are the tricks you hear about, but to emphasise their delusory quality is a distortion. There will of course be some out-and-out abuses, but advertisers and manufacturers of pre-cooked food do have to be careful about the conformity of their public image to the contents of their packages.[26] In any event the presentation of a picture of the foodstuff itself has frequently come to give way to depictions of alluring background contexts (margarine set against the pastoral countryside), or of narratives whose stories tempt the user (to use a stock cube to save time). The manipulative semiology of these food-related presentations is far more sophisticated and long-reaching than the substitution of green paper for a lettuce leaf.[27]

Designers of cook-books appear to have dabbled in this trickery area for a while, but many large concerns such as *Time-Life,* under the influence of Richard Olney in the early 1970s, effected a revolution in food presentation by insisting on natural products and the presentation of edible dishes. It is rare now to find a photographer of cookery-books who will admit to anything more than minimal 'enhancing' of the food.[28] Significantly the focus has also shifted away from always photographing the food or dish, to photographing suggestive environments such as holiday landscapes (food is a passport to escape), restaurant scenes (food is a way out of housekeeping or food means having money), the great chef (food is fame). With an increasing consciousness of the swiftly changing bases for the recognition of status, an early 1970s' reluctance to include people in pictures because their clothes and fashions would date a book, is being replaced by an acceptance of the need to appeal to the immediate audience by depicting them.[29] Where food is shown it is often presented artfully arranged on hexagonal dishes (food as designer life-style), and this end effect is also geared toward a message about 'food as a status symbol'. Just what form that status takes is variable and depends on the class, race and gender of the targeted audience.[30]

Furthermore, many cook-book publishers realised early that the complete colour photograph comic was not relaxing for the reader, and that it gave the impression of little substance. In the mid-1960s *The Robert Carrier Cookbook*[31] gleaned from Carrier's magazine experience at *Harper's Bizarre, Vogue* and *The Sunday Times,* presented an intelligent combination of full-colour photograph still-lifes of food such as 'Farmhouse Apple Pie', with many detailed drawings by Charles Pickard that were both decorative and helpful. Some earlier blockbuster cook-books, such as *Betty Crocker's New Picture Book* (1961)[32] had used both drawings and photographs; the latter were mainly for food while the drawings were restricted to illustration of 'life-style' in, for example, the happy nuclear family depicted over the title 'Meal Planning' (p.28). Later design-led publications continued to attempt a more serious, less 'flashy' approach by borrowing the developments in drawing from the Elizabeth David tradition and incorporating them into books which also included many photographs.

One mammoth example of this combination is *The*

Good Housekeeping Step-by-step Cook Book (1979)[33] which moved away from the tradition of using black and white photographs for the step-by-step techniques, to line-drawings. In fact the whole design-team process as described above was acted through, but then the best photograph of each step was chosen. The illustrator drew from the photographs, and the drawings were then returned to the designer so that areas of shading and tint (brown/grey) could be chosen. The aim of this *Good Housekeeping* edition was to illustrate every step and every dish. In the process a number of questions are raised about the value of the procedure: how many times do you need to show the stirring of dry ingredients in a bowl? – as well as questions about its possibility: a line-drawing is not that helpful for showing the consistency of custard or beaten egg.[34] Perhaps the totality of the aims of such books have instigated the recent movements away from the step-by-step approach.

In the current international book market arena, these big blockbuster cook-books are open to considerable manipulation. If a publisher knows that a book could sell 50,000 copies in the UK and 500,000 in the United States, then there are enormous pressures to design and illustrate the book for the US audience. There have been cases of the photography for a cook-book being undertaken primarily for the US edition, and the pictures having for economic reasons, to also be used for the British edition despite differences in ingredients, quantities or techniques. In some examples a recipe which was part of traditional British cooking and had to be included in the UK edition, was illustrated by a picture of an entirely different recipe from the US edition. Often the UK edition will attempt to make good the difference in the cultural perception of food simply by using a different cover. Indisputably books are frequently bought by their covers.

Design-led publishing house productions arose both

from the need to develop and sophisticate techniques of photographic illustration made available by new technology, and from the emergence of vast publishing markets which were simultaneously created and satisfied by that new technology. Of course the picture is far more complex, and rests on a web of social, economic, political and cultural changes. Yet the design-led book in its need to appeal broadly provides a clear example of corporate production. The extensive dependence on illustration means that there may not be a recognisable 'author'. Rather there are series editors, section editors and subeditors, ensuring the consistency of any written material and the compatibility of text and illustration. Superficially there could be much of benefit here to new working patterns. But rather than developing a collective pattern of discussion, argument, agreement and constructive dissension, there is instead an overwhelming need to achieve corporate identity, apparent consensus, the bland easing of lives into acceptable patterns. By and large those patterns appear to be deeply rooted in economic relations of the food industry and the politics of food.

Cookery-books, even cookery texts for schools, have always been an invitation to a particular life-style, to patterns of living which are not familiar. You do not buy a book to learn how to cook something you already know how to cook. Despite the claims that one reads Elizabeth David because of the quality of her prose, what distinguishes writers like her from most travel writers is that she introduces us to new foodstuffs, new techniques and new approaches to food. Everyday cookery knowledge used to be transmitted orally. Now wherever that tradition has died the market supplies pre-cooked food, packaged food, fast food and instant food to fill the gap, and advertising, by and large, instructs us in how to eat it: for example we are insistently told that breakfast should consist of fruit juice, cereal and coffee. Cookery-books of whatever kind are an invitation to take on different patterns, but the activity of that invitation is various. The readers may be led in to food that conforms to a broad social picture as with much magazine and in-house publishing work; they may be titillated by evanescent designer-difference: foods that look radically foreign and appeal to the sense of 'belonging to a club'; or they may be asked to think carefully about far-reaching change in their eating patterns because of diet, foodstuffs or food preparation.[35]

In these times, the type of invitation offered is often coded primarily in the illustrations. I would like to end with a cautionary tale to readers, writers, publishers and designers: the case of the newly illustrated *Italian Food*[36] by Elizabeth David. Reactions to this book have been curiously violent and oddly polarised. Due to certain publishing problems,[37] but also to Elizabeth David's interest in and knowledge of fine art, the 1987 edition dropped the original drawings by Guttuso and took the opportunity to display a wide range of Italian paintings of food and food-related illustration. David herself made the point that the choice was deliberately not from the well-known Old Masters but from among the so-called second rank: the paintings which are recognised to be well executed, technically interesting but which, possibly because they cannot satisfy the public's need for narrative in the way that portrait and landscape can because we have been told the history of the latter more consistently, are rarely anthologised and even more rarely shown. In effect what happens is that this book provides them with a necessary context which brings their depictions vividly into play. The book is an extraordinarily intelligent mixture of media in which each enhances the other.

However, this text in its earlier printing had a specific form as a book, an object with its own invitation. Earlier readers appear to have objected strenuously to the different invitation of the new edition.[38] This may simply be a case of habit – a much-loved book has been changed, which is temporarily annoying in the way that a change in the layout of the daily newspaper can be annoying. There is also the element of taboo, since many of David's books have become cultural icons marking a renewed post-war interest in food which was and is part of post-colonial Britain. Changes to this kind of text are often seen as a desecration. Further there is the more general concept of an illustrated book as an object which should not be tampered with, in itself a hangover from the days when the supposed mechanical invariability of the printed book gave it an authority as a fixed text. But in this case, possibly more relevant, the new edition is so highly illustrated with colour plates that it transgresses into the field of the corporate publisher. Superficially, the object appears to duplicate the techniques of the manufactured coffee-table books which are there to decorate the living-room, and not to be read with any attention.

The design-led books and the variety of new approaches to illustration of books by individual writers, have both been responses to the recent developments in the technology of printing and publishing. As with all new technological developments, it will take time for the producers as well as for the audience to assess the implications for our understanding of representation. For the moment each genre of illustration demonstrates a quite different kind of invitation to the reader, yet each can also provide the other with resources of great potential for the realisation of cultural imagination.

Notes and References

1. E. David, *A book of Mediterranean Food* (London, 1950).
2. *Good Housekeeping's Picture Cookery* (London, 1951).
3. *Good Housekeeping Cookery Book*, ed. F. Jack (London, 1925).
4. E. Ayrton, *Good Simple Cookery* (Hurst and Blackett, 1958).
5. M. Patten, *A to Z Cookery in Colour* (London, 1963).
6. M. Patten, *Step-by-step Cookery* (London, 1963).
7. N. Spain, *The Colour Cookery Book* (Manchester, 1963).
8. Much of the information about the illustrations to Elizabeth

David's books which follows in this essay was gained from an interview kindly given by the writer and from a subsequent written communication.

9. E. David, *French Country Cooking* (London, 1951).
10. E. David, *Italian Food* (London, 1954).
11. P. Gray and P. Boyd, *Plats du Jour* (Penguin, 1957).
12. A. Toklas, *The Alice B. Toklas Cook Book* (London, 1954).
13. D. Seton, *Essentials of Modern Cookery* (London, 1945).
14. This and the following editions are: *Essentials of Modern Cookery* (London, 1956), *Cookery with the Professional Touch* (London, 1957), and *Dora Seton's Cookery Book* (London, 1965).
15. B. Nilson, *The Career Woman's Cookbook* (London, 1966).
16. Much of the following information was gleaned from a telephone interview kindly given by the writer, several months before her untimely death.
17. At an earlier stage in her career, Grigson worked for the publishers Thames and Hudson; and she claims a continuing interest in design, not the least through a son-in-law who is a typographer.
18. Most of the material provided by Alan Davidson in the following paragraphs was gained from two interviews kindly given by the writer.
19. A. Davidson, *North Atlantic Seafood* (London, 1979).
20. A. Davidson, *Mediterranean Seafood* (London, 1972) and *Seafood of South-East Asia* (Singapore, 1976).
21. A. Davidson, *Fasting and Feasting* (London, 1988).
22. From an interview with Vicky Hayward, food editor of Weidenfeld and Nicholson.
23. From an interview with designer Deborah Mackinnon.
24. See R. Coward, *Female Desire* (London, 1984).
25. From a written communication by food writer and editor Elizabeth Driver.
26. The Advertising Standards Authority ensure a considerable degree of faithfulness between illustration and contents.
27. This kind of manipulation has been recognised, even academically, for some time by writers such as Roland Barthes in the essay 'Ornamental Cookery', *Mythologies* (Granada, 1973/1957), or Marshall McLuhan in his *Dewline Newsletters* from the late 1960s.
28. Some time was spent looking through the photographic libraries of food photographers, but none of those consulted would comment on whether or not they had been involved in such manipulation.
29. Comment from V. Hayward, as above.
30. See for example E. Mickler, *White Trash Cooking* (Berkeley, 1966).
31. R. Carrier, *The Robert Carrier Cookbook* (London, 1965).
32. *Betty Crocker's New Picture Book* (London, 1961).
33. *The Good Housekeeping Step-by-step Cook Book* (London, 1979).
34. E. Driver, as above.

35. The growing anthropological literature on food-related customs indicates a new awareness of some of these questions.
36. E. David, *Italian Food* (London, 1987).
37. David mentions these in the introduction to the 1987 edition.
38. See for example the review by C. Reid, 'Coffee table cuisine', *Times Literary Supplement* (April 15–21, 1988), p. 342.

Index

Adam, Robert 49-50
alms-dish 12
Arab cookery 15, 17-8, 20ff
assays 10-12
Audiger (*La Maison Reglée* 1692)
    108-9

backstools 41, 52
Baghdad Cookery Book (1226)
    18,19, 20, 23
boars's head 14
Bradley, Martha (*The British
    Housewife*, Vol. 1, c 1760) 112,
    115
breakfast room 51

cabinets 48
canopies 8, 31-2, 35, 37
Carter, Charles (*The Compleat
    City and Country Cook* 1732)
    112-3
Celtic eating habits 5-8
chairs 8, 30, 34-5, 38, 46-9
chargers 82-6
cookery books 108ff, 141, 155-6
croquettes 129, 133
cup-boards 9, 31-2, 38-9, 45

David, Elizabeth (*A Book of Medi-
    terranean Food* 1950) 142, 147;
    (*French Country Cooking*
    1951) 147; (*Italian Food* 1987
    edn.) 157

Davidson, Alan 149-50
Dawson, Thomas (*Good
    Huswife's Jewell* 1596) 91
delftware 77-8, 82-4
dining parlour 43, 45, 58
dining room 43-5, 47-8, 50, 53
    diner à la Russe 131, 134-5
doily 135, 136-7
dumb-waiter 50-1

etiquette 29
ewers, ewery 9-10, 60, 94-6

fireplace 34, 51
food colouring 16-26
food rationing 147
forks 69, 72-4
Forme of Cury (c 1390) 16, 28, 99
Francatelli, Charles (*A Plain
    Cookery Book for the Working
    Classes* 1852) 132
frumenty 20

garnishing 23, 91-3
gender 138
gentility 137-9
Glasse, Hannah (*Art of Cookery*
    1747) 112, 121, 123
gold 18-9
Good Housekeeping 142-5, 155
Gourmet (1950) 145
Great Chamber 33-43, 60, 100
Great Hall 29-33, 36

161

Index

Grigson, Jane 149-51

Ham House 46-7, 52
handwashing 9
Hardwick Hall 40-1, 43
Hepplewhite 49
high table 8-9, 30
Holkham MS 100
Holme, Randle (*The Academy of Armoury* 1688) 45-7, 49, 90
Howard, Henry (*England's Newest Way* 1708) 109, 111-2

knives 67-8, 70-2

Lamb, Patrick (*Royal Cookery* 1710) 89, 117
Life and Death of Sir Henry Unton (National Portrait Gallery) 74, 89

Markham, Gervase (*The English Huswife* 1615) 1-2, 87
Massialot, F (*The Court and Country Cook* 1702) 108-10
May, Robert (*The Accomplisht Cook* 1665) 107
mediaeval feast rituals 8-13
Ménagier de Paris (1393) 19
menus 98-121
minstrels 12
murree (mulberry pottage) 24
Murrell, John (*A New Booke of Cookerie* 1615) 91, 106

napkins 64-66

parsley 20-21, 143
peacock 14
Perfect School of Instructions for Officers of the Mouth (1682) 64-5
Poseidonios 5-8
pottages 13, 16, 24
pottery 65, 76-8, 82-7
precedence 28, 37
publishing 112, 141-4, 155-9

reward table 12

Russell, John (*Boke of Nurture* c 1450) 101

saffron 17, 19-22, 25
salads 92-3
salt, salt cellar 9, 61-5
serving 9ff, 79-81
Seton, Dora (*Essentials of Modern Cookery* 1945) 148
sgraffito 85-6
side tables 44-5, 49-50
sippets 92
slipware 83, 85-6
Smith, E (*The Compleat Housewife* 1727) 112, 114
sotelties 14-5, 133
Soyer, Alexis (*The Modern Housewife* 1849) 130-3
spoons 66-7
stools 9, 38
sugar sculpture 14
surnappe 10, 12

tables 30, 38, 44-8, 50; breakfast tables 51; tea tables 52; table plan 89, 131, 134; table setting 90, 109-20; table decoration 134-5; see also reward table, side table
tablecloths 9, 59-61
tapestries 29-32, 37-8, 42, 47
tarts 25
tea 51-3
testers and canopies 31-2, 35, 37
trenchers 70-1, 74-6

upholstery 40, 46-7
urchins 16

Viandier 16, 21
Victorian cookery 123-40

wallpaper 50
Whole Duty of a Woman (1737) 112-3
Worde, Wynkyn de (*Book of Kervynge* 1508) 59, 61, 65, 74, 94
wriggled work 70-1, 76, 82